The MAILBOX®
The Education Center®

Sensational Centers

grades PreK–K

P9-EGN-668

Over **150** center activities for your favorite themes!

- Art
- Blocks
- Cooking
- Discovery

- Dramatic play
- Literacy
- Manipulatives
- Math

- Motor
- Music and movement
- Science
- Sensory

Organized by seasonal themes!

Managing Editor: Brenda Miner

Editorial Team: Becky S. Andrews, Diane Badden, Kimberley Bruck, Karen A. Brudnak, Kitty Campbell, Valerie R. Corbeille, Pam Crane, Roxanne LaBell Dearman, Susan DeRiso, Lynette Dickerson, Sandra Faulkner, Theresa Lewis Goode, Karen Brewer Grossman, Tazmen Hansen, Marsha Heim, Lori Z. Henry, Julie A. Koczur, Debra Liverman, Kim Love, Dorothy C. McKinney, Thad H. McLaurin, Audrey McNeill, Suzanne Moore, Sharon Murphy, Jennifer Nunn, Mark Rainey, Mackie Rhodes, Kim Richman, Greg D. Rieves, Hope Rodgers, Rebecca Saunders, Barry Slate, Donna K. Teal, Dayle Timmons, Zane Williard

www.themailbox.com

Manufactured in the United States
10 9 8 7 6 5 4 3 2

Table of Contents

Centers at a Glance

Themes	Art	Block	Cooking	Discovery	Dramatic Play	Listening	Literacy	Math	Manipulatives	Motor	Music/Movement	Science	Sensory
Apples	5		7		6		4	5		6		7	4
Birthday	8			10	9		9	8					10
Leaves	13					13	12	14				14	12
Fire Safety	17	19	19		18		16	16				17	18
Pumpkins	22						20	22		20		21	21
Farm	26						24	24		26		25	25
Turkeys	30				30		29	28				28	29
Transportation	32	34		32			33	33		34			
Gingerbread			38		38		36	36		37			37
Shapes	43	42		41			40		40	42	43		41
Penguins	46	46		45			44	44					45
Mittens				48	50		48	50		49			49
Dinosaurs	52			52	53		53	54					54
Teeth	56			58			57	56	57		58		
Hearts	62			61			62	60		61			60
Nursery Rhymes		65	66	65			66	64					64
Eggs	70						68, 69	68			70		69
Bunnies	74		74	72			72	73					73
Rain	78						76	76		78		77	77
Frogs	82		82				81	80				80	81
Garden	85				86		84	84	85				86
Butterflies	89		90				88	88		90		89	
Pets		93			93		94	94	92	92			
Picnic	98				97		96	98	96				97
Stars	101		102				100	100		102			101
Zoo	105						105	106		104		106	104
Teddy Bears	110						108	108			110	109	109

Apples All Around

Invite your little ones to sink their teeth into these handpicked apple centers.

"Apple-tizing" Apples

Literacy Center

▶ print awareness
▶ letter matching
▶ left-to-right progression

Glue pictures or drawings of apple food items to a large apple cutout as shown; then label each picture. Place the cutout at a center along with a small basket of letter manipulatives. When a child visits the center, have him use the letters to form a word from the cutout. After "reading" the word, have him put the letters back in the basket and then continue in the same manner with the remaining words on the cutout.

Worm Workout

Sensory Center

▶ tactile exploration
▶ fine motor

It's time to give some worms a workout as your youngsters explore different textures! In advance, cut a supply of rubber bands so they resemble worms and obtain several bags of dried apple chips. Put the worms in a plastic bowl and spread the apple chips on a baking sheet. Place the items at a center. Invite each child to make the worms crawl, hide, race, and tunnel through the apple chips. Whew! These worms are really moving!

Worms in My Apple!

Using this center idea is a great way to wiggle positional concepts into your curriculum! To prepare, paint a medium-size foam ball with a mixture of one part glue to two parts paint. When the paint is dry, use a pencil to poke two holes through the ball (apple); then use a permanent marker to outline each hole as shown. Fashion a stem and leaf using pipe cleaners and push them into the top of the apple. To make worms, bend long pipe cleaners in half; then twist them together. Place the items at a center. Invite each pair of students to take turns placing the worms *in, out, over, under, beside, around,* and *through* the apple as directed by his partner. Look at those worms go!

Through!

Math Center

positional words ◀
following directions ◀

Apple-Part Art

Here's a painting project that will result in an orchard of apple trees! Simply core several apples and then cut the cores in half as shown. Cut the remainders of the apples into thick slices. Place the apple parts at a center along with a class supply of white construction paper and shallow pans of brown, green, and red paint. To make an apple tree, a child first dips an apple slice into the brown paint and then presses it onto a sheet of paper to form a trunk. Using a different apple slice and green paint, she repeats this process to paint the leaves. Next, she dips the flat end of the core into the red paint and then presses it among the leaves to create apples. When the paint is dry, display students' apple trees on a bulletin board.

Art Center

creative expression ◀
fine motor ◀

Apple Dough Twists

Apple dough is an "a-peel-ing" way to strengthen your little ones' fingers! In advance, follow the recipe below to make a batch of apple play dough; then place it at a center along with a baking sheet. Invite each child to roll two portions of dough between his fingers to make ropes. Next, have him press one end of each rope together and then twist them. Encourage him to place the apple twists on the baking sheet and pretend to bake them. They smell yummy!

Apple dough is an "a-peel-ing" way to strengthen your little ones' fingers! In advance, follow the recipe below to make a batch of apple play dough; then place it at a center along with a baking sheet. Invite each child to roll two portions of dough between his fingers to make ropes. Next, have him press one end of each rope together and then twist them. Encourage him to place the apple twists on the baking sheet and pretend to bake them. They smell yummy!

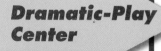

Motor Center

▶ fine motor
▶ following directions

Apple Dough

Ingredients:
2 c. flour
1 c. salt
1 c. apple juice
several drops of red, yellow, or green food coloring

Directions:
Mix the ingredients together in a large bowl. Add more flour or juice as needed until the desired consistency is achieved.

Apples With Character

Your youngsters will shine with pride as they create apple characters to use during pretend play! Simply place a variety of real or foam apples at a center along with a selection of Mr. Potato Head® parts. Encourage each child to use the toy parts to create an apple character. Then invite him to use his prop to tell a story. As he does, he'll have the opportunity to strengthen his language skills. Now that's a happy ending!

Dramatic-Play Center

▶ oral language
▶ creative expression
▶ fine motor

Once upon a time there were two apples...

who lived with their granny.

Apple Bowls

These edible bowls can hold almost any snack! In advance, create a class supply of apple bowls by cutting apples in half and then scooping out the center of each apple half. Dip the bowls in lemon juice and place them at a center along with plastic spoons, yogurt, and toppings such as sprinkles and cinnamon. When a child visits the center, she fills her bowl with yogurt and then adds a topping. You're sure to hear lots of crunching and munching as your little ones eat their entire snacks—including the bowls!

Cooking Center

sensory exploration ◄
decision making ◄

Apple Bubble Blowers

Involve your students in discovering how an apple can be used to make beautiful bubble paintings. In advance, follow the recipe below to make a batch of colorful bubble mixture. Pour the mixture into a shallow pan and place it at a center along with a class supply of cored apples (see illustration) and a class supply of white construction paper. When a child visits this center, she grasps an apple with both hands and dips one end into the bubble mixture. Then she lifts the apple and blows through the other end so that the bubbles pop onto a sheet of paper, creating a colorful print. This apple center is sure to be popular!

Science Center

investigating ◄
cause and effect
creative expression ◄

Colorful Bubble Mixture

In each pan mix:
5 tbsp. soft water (or distilled)
4 tbsp. clear Dawn® dish detergent
5 or more drops of a different food coloring

It's a Birthday Bash!

Wrap the presents, light the candles, and put on your party clothes. It's birthday party time and everyone is invited!

Math Center

▶ *matching numerals to corresponding sets*
▶ *counting*

How Many Candles?

Here's an activity that adds up to counting skills worth celebrating! Simply stock a center with cupcake liners, play dough, a supply of index cards numbered from 1 to 15, and 15 birthday candles. When a child visits the center, he fills a liner with play dough to resemble a cupcake. Next, he selects a card and puts the matching number of candles on the cupcake. To continue play, he removes the candles and then repeats the activity using different number cards. Now that's counting fun!

Art Center

▶ *fine motor*
▶ *following directions*

Hats Off to Birthdays!

Celebrate little ones' creativity with these festive party hats! In advance, stock a center with lengths of curling ribbon, tape, a class supply of 9" x 12" sheets of construction paper, a shallow pan of thinned glue, large paintbrushes, confetti, a stapler, a hole puncher, and pipe cleaners. To make a hat, a child tapes several lengths of ribbon onto a sheet of construction paper as shown. Next, she paints a layer of glue on the opposite side and then sprinkles the paper with confetti. When the glue is dry, help her form a cone shape to resemble a hat; then staple it in place. Punch a hole in each of the two bottom corners. Insert a pipe cleaner through each hole; then twist to secure. Invite youngsters to put on their hats and loosely twist the pipe cleaners around their chins. That's quite a party hat!

The Icing on the Cake

At this center, reading success is icing on the cake! In advance, program a card with "Happy Birthday" and a supply of student name cards similar to the ones shown. Make a construction paper copy of the cake pattern on page 11. Cut it out; then laminate it. Place these items at the center along with several sheets of edible decorating letters. To decorate a cake pattern, a child uses the birthday card and his name card as a guide to spell a birthday message. Happy birthday to…everyone!

Literacy Center

left-to-right ◀
progression
letter matching ◀

HAPPY BIRTHDAY JADE

JADE

SEAN

HAPPY BIRTHDAY

Let's Bake a Cake!

Little ones are sure to be busy at this pretend bakery! In advance, ask a local bakery to donate several empty cake boxes. Place them in your dramatic-play area along with play dough, a variety of baking utensils, markers, notepads, and play money. For added hands-on fun, provide faux cake decorations, such as magnetic letters and artificial flower tops. Now invite students to take turns ordering and making birthday cakes. Whew! This bakery is busy!

Dramatic-Play Center

role-playing ◀
cooperation ◀

ORDER

9

A Lot of Air

Use this activity to involve your youngsters in experimenting with motion! To prepare, use masking tape to create a starting line and a finish line at a center tabletop. Stock the center with party items of various weights, such as a paper plate, a wrapped box, and a cupcake liner. When a child visits the center, have her place an object on the starting line and then try to blow it across the finish line. After she tests the objects, have her sort them into two piles based on whether they blew across the finish line or not. One, two, three—blow!

Discovery Center

▶ *exploring motion*
▶ *sorting*

START

FINISH

What's Inside the Birthday Bag?

Sensory Center

▶ *tactile discrimination*
▶ *critical thinking*

Pique your youngsters' curiosity with these mystery birthday bags! In advance, fill your sensory table with tissue paper and colorful recycled gift bags. Place a different party item, such as a plastic spoon or a birthday candle, in each bag. Then cover each object with a piece of crumpled tissue paper. When a child visits the center, have her use her sense of touch to guess the contents of each bag. Next, have her peek inside the bag to check her guess. Surprise! It's a spoon!

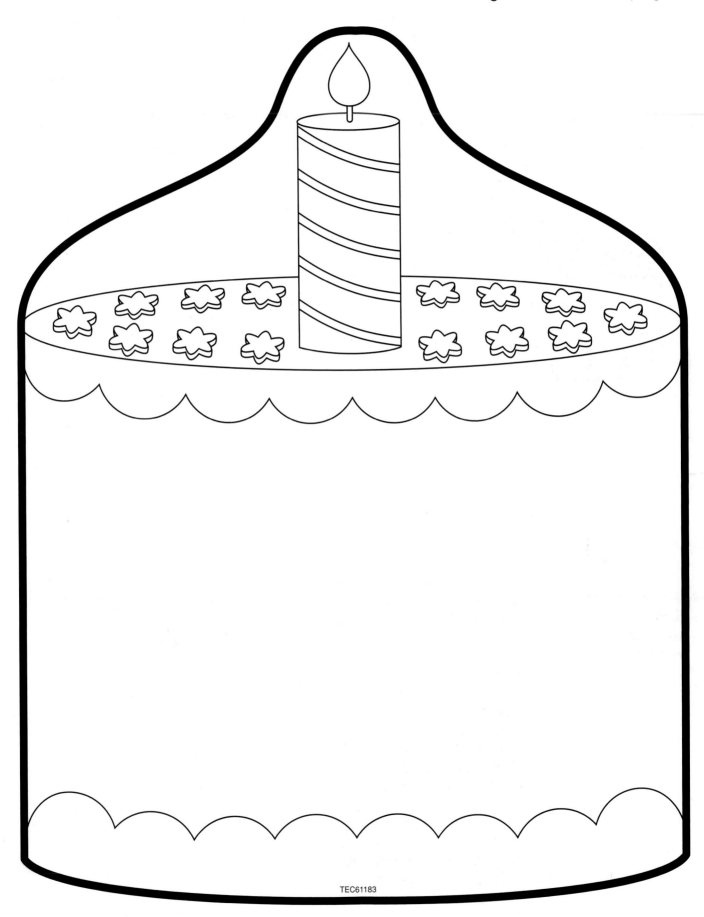

TEC61183

Lots of Leaves!

Jump right into a pile of autumn-related activities with these "unbe-leaf-able" centers!

Jump In!

Get little ones involved in patterning practice using layers of lovely fall leaves! Simply half-fill a wading pool (or sensory table) with a variety of real leaves. As each child visits the center, have her sort the leaves by shape, color, or size. Then have her use the sorted leaves to make patterns. What fantastic fall foliage fun!

Sensory Center

▶ visual discrimination
▶ sorting
▶ patterning

Piles and Piles of Leaves

Rake up some fall fun for your youngsters with this literacy idea! In advance, make 20 construction paper copies of the leaf patterns on page 15; then cut them out. Program each of five paper lunch bags with a different letter. Next, cut out magazine pictures of items that begin with the letter on each bag. If desired, include some extra pictures that do not match any of the bags. Glue each picture on a leaf cutout. Place these items at a center along with a toy rake. When a child visits the center, have him scatter the leaves and then rake them into a pile. Next, have him sort the leaves by naming each picture and putting it into the matching bag. For younger children, simply scatter leaves with labeled pictures; then encourage your students to "read" each picture.

Literacy Center

▶ phonemic awareness
▶ letter-sound association
▶ vocabulary development

Five Fluttering Leaves

Flitter, flutter! Youngsters are sure to be whisked away by this listening center activity! In advance, make a recording of the poem below. Place the recording and five real or paper leaves at a center. Then recite the poem with your students. Invite each child to visit the center and act out the poem as she listens to the recording. If desired, print the poem on sentence strips and have students sequence them as they listen to the poem. Watch out for falling leaves!

Listening Center

listening ◀
following ◀
directions

Five Fluttering Leaves

Five fall leaves,
Green is what they wore.
One fluttered to the ground.
Now there are four.

Four fall leaves
Are as big as they can be.
The rain washes one away.
Now there are three.

Three fall leaves,
Turning colors in the dew.
The wind blows one away.
Now there are two.

Two fall leaves,
Hanging in the sun.
One lets go.
Now there is one.

One last leaf—
Now its time is done.
It flips and flutters to the ground.
Now there are none.

Splattered With Fall Colors

This art activity will add an array of autumn colors to your classroom! In advance, gather a class supply of real leaves. Use rolled tape to secure each leaf to the center of a 9" x 12" sheet of white construction paper. Place the papers at a center along with a shallow box and several spray bottles of thinned red, yellow, and orange paint. When a child visits the center, have her place a paper in the box (leaf side up) and then use the bottles to spray-paint her paper. When the paint is dry, carefully remove the leaf. Display both the splattered leaves and the colorful outlines to make a fantastic fall bulletin board. Look at those autumn hues!

Art Center

fine motor ◀
creative expression ◀

13

Math
Center

▶ *counting*

Falling for Leaves

Little ones will gather up counting skills with this leafy activity! Place a large die, a supply of small paper leaves, and one copy of the tree pattern on page 15 at a center. Have each child who visits the center place all of the leaves on the tree. Next, have him roll the die, count the dots, and remove the corresponding number of leaves from the tree. When the tree is bare, the activity is complete. Ooooh! Cooler weather is coming!

Fabulous Fall Leaves

Science
Center

▶ *observation*
▶ *creative expression*
▶ *fine motor*

Orange, yellow, red, and brown—autumn leaves are all around! To prepare for this science center, duplicate a class supply of construction paper leaves using the leaf patterns on page 15. Place the leaves at the center along with a variety of real leaves. Also provide magnifying glasses, a class supply of six-inch plastic-wrap squares, and squeezable bottles of red and yellow paint. When a child visits the center, have her use a magnifying glass to observe the veins in the real autumn leaves. Then have her squirt a small amount of each color of paint onto a paper leaf. Next, have her place a piece of plastic wrap over her painted leaf and crinkle the wrap. When the paint is dry, have the child remove the plastic wrap to reveal a colorful leaf with realistic-looking veins!

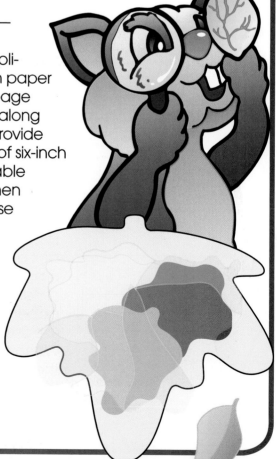

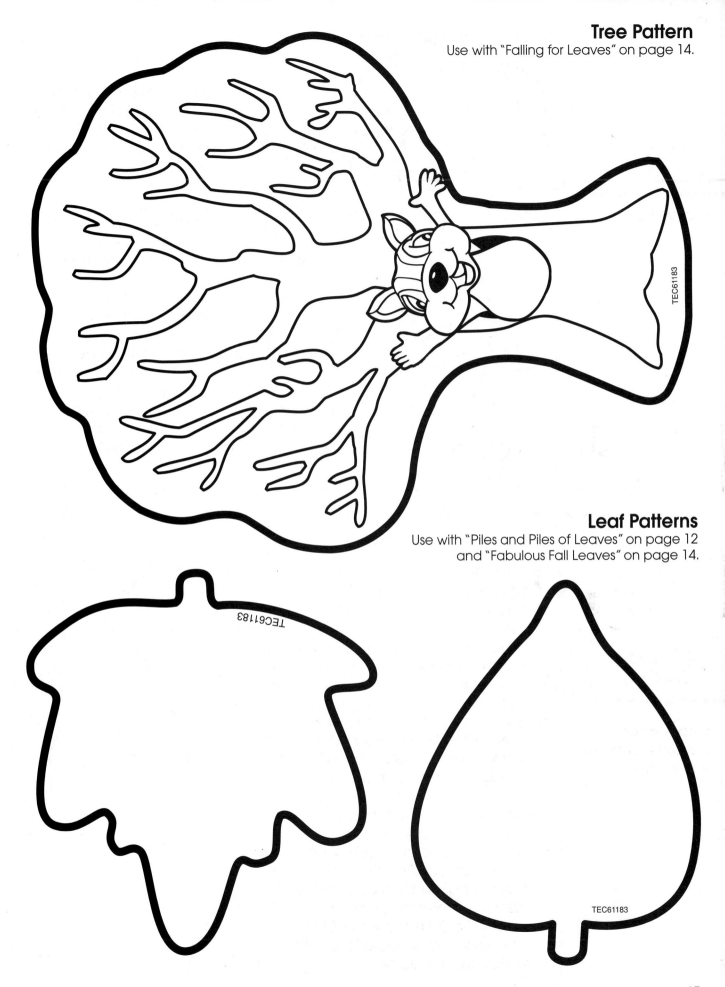

Tree Pattern
Use with "Falling for Leaves" on page 14.

TEC61183

Leaf Patterns
Use with "Piles and Piles of Leaves" on page 12 and "Fabulous Fall Leaves" on page 14.

TEC61183

TEC61183

Fire Safety First!

Your youngsters are sure to learn important emergency skills as they enjoy a swift ride through these fire safety centers.

Hot Hide-and-Seek

Your little ones will develop a flair for word recognition with this prereading activity. To prepare, print "fire" on several index cards using uppercase and lowercase letters and different text styles. Place the cards at the center along with your favorite fire safety books. Invite each child to choose one card and one book. Then encourage her to use the card to help her find the word *fire* throughout the book. If desired, ask her to count the number of times she finds the word.

Literacy Center

▶ *word recognition*
▶ *print awareness*

fire   FIRE   **fire**

Fire Hose Lineup

Size up your youngsters' discrimination skills with this math center. Cut drinking straws into five different lengths (one, two, three, four, and five inches) so that there is one of each length for each child. Then sort the straws by size into five separate containers. Place the containers, clear tape, and a class supply of 6" x 9" sheets of construction paper at a center. Direct each child to arrange the straws (fire hoses) in order from largest to smallest on a sheet of paper and then secure each one with tape. Now that's quite a lineup!

Math Center

▶ *size discrimination*
▶ *seriation*

Firefighters' Footwear

Why do firefighters wear rubber boots? Have your little ones put this question to the test with this water experiment. In advance, gather a plastic tub, a water-filled spray bottle, and several different kinds of material squares (such as nylon, wool, rubber, canvas, and fleece). Encourage a child to predict which fabrics will *absorb* the water and which fabrics will *repel* the water. Have the child test her predictions by placing each piece of fabric into the tub. Then invite her to spray water onto the fabric pieces and observe the results. So that's why firefighters wear rubber boots!

Science Center

observation skills ◀
predicting ◀
outcomes
fine motor ◀

Shapely Fire Engines

Shape up youngsters' visual discrimination skills with these fun fire engines. To prepare, make several tagboard templates in different shapes. Place the shapes along with construction paper, scissors, glue, and crayons at a center. Post a picture of a fire engine for youngsters to observe. Then invite a child to create his own fire engine. (For younger students, precut the construction paper shapes.) Have him arrange the shapes and then glue them onto a sheet of construction paper. My, that's a shapely fire engine!

Art Center

shapes ◀
creativity ◀

Flames Out!

Turn your dramatic-play center into a practice zone for this fire safety technique. Place a mat or carpet on the floor near this center and add a sturdy sign with the word FIRE. Then encourage pairs of students to visit the center. Ask one student to hold up the sign while the other practices putting out the flames by acting out "Stop, Drop, and Roll." What a valuable lifesaving lesson!

Fire Hose Fill-Up

Your little firefighters are sure to enjoy pouring and exploring water with imaginary fire hoses. Display plastic funnels, plastic pitchers, and several different lengths of clear plastic tubing at a water table. If desired, add glitter to the water to emphasize visual discrimination. Next, invite a child to attach a funnel to a piece of tubing and then pour water into the funnel. For added fun, have him tie a knot in the middle of a piece of tubing. Again, invite him to pour water into the tube. Have him watch what happens after each pouring.

Dalmatian Pup Cups

What's white with black spots? This delicious yogurt treat that has students practicing measurement skills! To prepare, gather a large carton of vanilla yogurt, a package of mini chocolate chips, a half-cup measure, a tablespoon, and a class supply of clear plastic cups and spoons. Place these items at a center along with colorful permanent markers. Instruct each child to use a marker to draw a dalmatian puppy face onto his plastic cup as shown. To make a treat, a child simply measures a half-cup of yogurt into his cup and then stirs in two tablespoons of chocolate chips. Yum! It's chow time!

Cooking Center

following directions ◄
measuring ◄
fine motor ◄

Fire Station Setup

Build cooperation skills as youngsters construct their very own fire station. Stock a block center with toys, such as fire trucks, people, ladders, bells, and a dalmatian dog. Invite a small group of youngsters to work together to build a fire station that has windows, doors, and a garage. As they play, encourage the group to use related vocabulary, such as *siren, alarm, fire extinguisher,* and *exit.* Brring! Brring! Sound the alarm!

Block Center

fine motor ◄
verbal skills ◄
cognitive skills ◄
cooperation ◄

It's Pumpkin Patch Time!

Enrich your youngsters' harvest spirit with this plentiful patch of pumpkin ideas!

Ooey-Gooey Pumpkin Pal

Motor Center

▶ tactile exploration
▶ fine motor

What's the scoop on pumpkin fun? This simple fine-motor activity! To make a pumpkin pal, use a permanent marker to draw a pumpkin outline on a large resealable bag. Next, squirt a dollop of shaving cream and a small amount of orange tempera paint into the bag. Seal the bag and use clear packaging tape to reinforce the seal. Invite a child to squish and squeeze the bag until an orange color appears. Next, have her use her finger to trace the pumpkin outline. Then encourage her to draw silly faces.

Jack-o'-Letters

Literacy Center

▶ letter matching
▶ following directions

Youngsters feel like blue-ribbon winners when they use these plump pumpkins to match letters! In advance, cut out nine construction paper copies of the pumpkin and triangle patterns on page 23. Use a marker to print a different letter on each pumpkin eye and nose (leave the last nose blank). Then print a corresponding letter on each triangle piece. On the 27th triangle, print *Happy Halloween* (or *Happy Harvest*). Place the triangles inside a plastic pumpkin pail. Then invite a child to match the letters until each pumpkin face is complete.

How Does Your Pumpkin Grow?

Cultivate an interest in pumpkins with this discovery activity. In advance, have parents donate ripened and unripened pumpkins. Place the pumpkins at the center along with green curling ribbon and artificial greenery to represent vines. When your little ones visit the pumpkin patch, encourage them to observe the pumpkins. Then have them sort the pumpkins by size and color. What's on the vine? Why, it's the great green pumpkin!

Science Center

visual discrimination ◄
sorting ◄

"Kool" Pumpkin Pies

Spice up the sensory center with the delicious scent of fresh pumpkin pie! Follow the recipe below to make a batch of scented play dough. Place the dough and mini aluminum pie pans at the sensory table. When a child visits the center, have her create pretend pumpkin pies. No tasting please!

Sensory Center

sensory experience ◄
fine motor ◄

No-Cook Kool-Aid® Play Dough

Ingredients:
2½ c. flour
½ c. salt
3 tbsp. cooking oil
1 tbsp. alum
3 tsp. ground cloves
1 c. boiling water
1 pkg. unsweetened Kool-Aid® (orange)
3 tsp. pumpkin pie spice

Directions:
Mix the ingredients in a large bowl. Add more flour or water until the desired consistency is achieved.

- number recognition
- counting
- one-to-one
  correspondence

Counting Teeth

Your youngsters will be all aglow when you treat them to this sweet math center! In advance, make ten construction paper copies of the pumpkin and hat patterns on page 23. Print a different numeral on each hat. Next, draw a different number of teeth on each pumpkin to correspond with the numeral on each hat. Cut out the hats and the pumpkins; then laminate them. Place them at your center along with a supply of candy corn cutouts. When a child visits the center, he matches a hat to the corresponding pumpkin and then places a candy corn cutout on each tooth. For younger children, glue each hat to its matching pumpkin and then have them practice number association by placing the corresponding number of candy corn cutouts on each pumpkin's teeth. What sweet success!

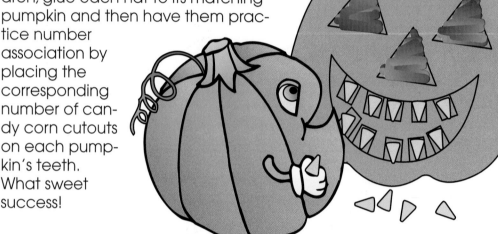

- fine motor
- creative expression

"Boo-tiful" Paper Cup Pumpkins

Get youngsters grinning from ear to ear when they decorate these unique pumpkins! To prepare, punch a small hole through the center of the bottom of one plastic cup for each child. To create a pumpkin, a child paints the outside of her cup with thinned glue; then she covers the glue with orange and yellow tissue paper squares. Next, she glues construction paper facial features to the inverted cup. When the glue dries, she inserts a green pipe cleaner into the punched-out hole (tape to secure if necessary) and then twists it to resemble a pumpkin vine. That's a festive pumpkin!

Pumpkin Pattern
Use with "Jack-o'-Letters" on page 20 and "Counting Teeth" on page 22.

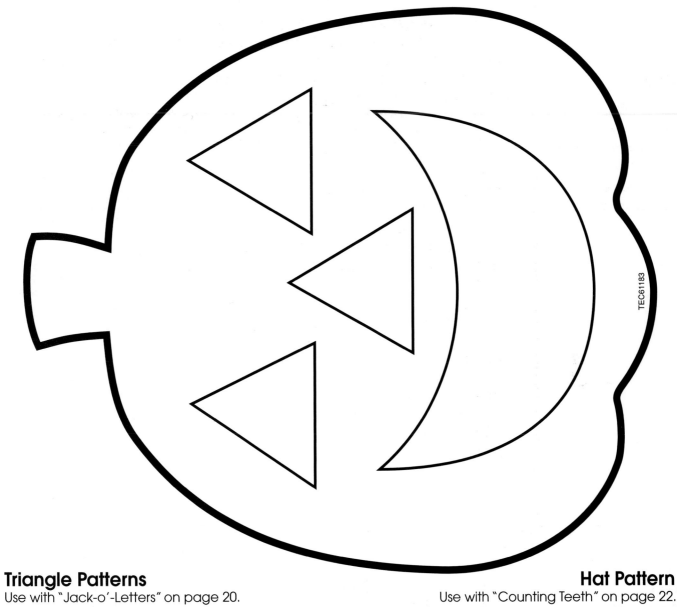

TEC61183

Triangle Patterns
Use with "Jack-o'-Letters" on page 20.

Hat Pattern
Use with "Counting Teeth" on page 22.

TEC61183

TEC61183

Farm Frolics!

Rise and shine! Head on down to the barn to feed some chickens, milk some cows, and practice some basic skills.

Literacy Center

▶ *creative writing*
▶ *rhyming*
▶ *creative expression*

I'm in the Rhyme!

Give your youngsters a chance to be the stars of their own nursery rhymes. During a group time, review favorite rhymes that relate to the farm, such as "Little Boy Blue," "Little Bo-Peep," or "Mary Had a Little Lamb." Then choose a language chunk from each rhyme and demonstrate how to personalize it for a child in your class. For example, "(Justin) had a little (goat)." Post sections of the traditional rhymes in your literacy center with blank spaces as shown. Then invite each child to visit the center and write or dictate his own rhyme on a large sheet of art paper. Then invite him to illustrate his new creation. Bind all the rhymes together for a new class book. Read the book aloud during your next circle time; then put it in the reading center for individual reading.

Justin had a little goat.

[_____] had a little [_____].

Math Center

▶ *number sequence*
▶ *number matching*

Gatherin' Eggs

It's off to the chicken coop to gather up some "egg-y" math skills. Use a permanent marker to label each of 12 Ping-Pong® balls (eggs) with a different number from 1 to 12. (For younger students, label the egg cups in a cleaned and sanitized egg carton with the numbers 1 to 12.) Store the eggs in a basket; then put the basket and empty egg carton in the math center. To complete the activity, invite an older child to put the eggs in numerical order and a younger student to match each egg to its corresponding egg cup.

Floating Feathers?

Gather your youngsters and have them brainstorm a list of animals that have feathers. Then have volunteers circle the animals on the list that are found on a farm. After the list is made, pass around realistic-looking craft feathers. Encourage youngsters to give descriptive words as they examine the feathers. Then pose this question: "Do feathers float?" Prepare two simple T graphs. On one, direct each child to clip a personalized clothespin to the side that indicates her prediction.

Provide a supply of feathers and a tub of water in your science center. Hang the second T graph nearby. Have each child complete the experiment and clip a clothespin on the second graph to indicate her results. After center time, compare the predicted results against the actual results. Wow, how friends of a feather flock together!

Science Center

critical thinking ◄
predicting ◄
experimenting ◄
comparing ◄

Here Chicky, Chicky!

Bang the pots and pans—it's feeding time! Explain to your little ones that a chicken's diet is made up mostly of corn. Show a few different examples of corn, such as popcorn kernels, popcorn, dried corn seed, and cornmeal. Then fill the sensory tub with actual chicken feed (for older students) or popcorn kernels (for younger students). Provide scoops, cups, and funnels for further exploration under adult supervision. Come and get it!

Sensory Center

exploration ◄
measurement ◄
fine motor ◄

▶ *creative expression*
▶ *color exploration*
▶ *fine motor*

"Udder-ly" Fun Art

Use rubber gloves to simulate milking a cow, and make some art in the process! Fill separate gloves with different colors of watered-down tempera paint. Knot each glove's opening; then poke a small hole in the ends of the gloves' index, middle, and ring fingers. Have each youngster use the gloves to squirt, drip, and drizzle paint designs onto a sheet of paper. Just "moo-velous"!

Sew and Sew

These cute lacing cards make practicing fine-motor skills a bushel of fun! To create the cards, duplicate the shapes on page 27 onto tagboard. Color the shapes, cut them out, and laminate them. Then use a hole puncher to make holes where indicated. Provide colorful shoestrings or lengths of yarn for youngsters to use to sew around the cards' edges. After a child has finished lacing, have him take out the shoestrings to ready the center for the next student. E-I-E-I-O!

▶ *fine motor*
▶ *visual discrimination*
▶ *hand-eye coordination*

TEC61183

TEC61183

TEC61183

Terrific Turkeys

Gobble, gobble! Your little ones are sure to learn more about turkeys as they visit the following terrific centers.

Math Center

▶ *patterning*
▶ *size discrimination*
▶ *oral language*

Nesting Numbers

Have your youngsters create "egg-citing" patterns with this clutch of eggs. To prepare, obtain a hula-hoop toy and a supply of small and large plastic eggs. Tell your little ones that turkey eggs are larger than chicken eggs. Then invite a small group to arrange the eggs in a pattern around the inside of the hoop. As they do, encourage them to describe the attributes they are using for patterning. You're sure to hear cheerful chants of "small egg, large egg, small egg, large egg!"

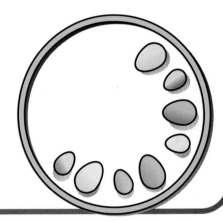

Science Center

▶ *fine motor*
▶ *sensory exploration*

Scratch the Surface

Exploration is just a scratch away with this simulation of an instinctive turkey trait. To prepare, add sand to a plastic tub along with a cup of dried corn and several sand scrapers. Explain to your little ones that a turkey uses its claws to scratch the ground in search of food (corn, nuts, seeds, and roots). Invite a child to use a scraper to scratch through the sand in search of the hidden kernels of corn. Dig in!

Turkey Treats

In celebration of the turkey, use its favorite food to help your youngsters with measurement exploration. Fill your sensory table with dried corn and a variety of plastic cups, funnels, and containers. Then invite your youngsters to measure and pour the corn into different containers. Wow! That's a whole lot of turkey treats!

Sensory Center

tactile experience ◄
measuring ◄
fine motor ◄
hand-eye ◄
coordination

Telling About Turkeys

My turkey has _eggs_ .
Name _Thomas_

Practicing prereading skills is a treat with these terrific turkey booklet pages! In advance, make a copy of page 31 for each child. Then program several index cards with turkey-related words and illustrations (feathers, wattle, caruncle, spurs, beard, eggs, etc.). Place these supplies at a center along with a nonfiction turkey book. Give each child a page and then ask him to choose one card. Have him write or dictate the word in the space provided on his page. Then ask him to illustrate his sentence. Later, combine the booklet pages into a class book for all to enjoy.

Literacy Center

left-to-right ◄
progression
creative thinking ◄

Turkey Strut

Dramatic-Play Center

▶ role-playing
▶ creative thinking
▶ gross motor

Encourage youngsters' imaginations with a stroll down to the turkey farm! Stock a center with farmer gear (straw hats, bandanas, vests), turkey gear (feather headbands, cone-shaped party hats for beaks), and plastic buckets that will hold imaginary turkey feed. Explain to youngsters that *poults* (baby turkeys) make a *cheep-cheep* and a *kee-kee-kee* sound. Further explain that a *hen yelps* and a *tom* says *gobble, gobble.* Invite several students to don the farmer gear while several others dress as turkeys. Have the farmers sprinkle some feed around on the ground and call the turkeys to dinner. Then encourage the little turkeys to strut, scratch, and peck at the ground in search of food as they make turkey sounds. If desired, play your favorite turkey–strutting music.

Kee-kee!

Feathery Friend

Art Center

▶ fine motor
▶ creative expression

"Wattle" you know—these funny bird paintings are sure to teach your youngsters about a turkey's body parts. In advance, collect several feathers, tempera paints, crayons, red tissue paper pieces, and orange yarn pieces. Mask out the sentence starter on a copy of page 31 and then make a class supply of copies. Place the supplies and a picture of a real turkey at a center. Invite each child to color her turkey's head and body. Next, have her glue a yarn *caruncle* on the top of its beak and a tissue paper *wattle* on its neck. Then have her dip a different feather into each paint color to brush on beautiful turkey feathers.

Name McKenna

My turkey has _____.

Name _____

On the Move!

Make the move to transportation studies with these hands-on learning centers!

Art Center

▶ *creative thinking*
▶ *fine motor*
▶ *classification*

By Water, Land, or Air

This art center results in a collaborative mural. In advance, prepare a background for the mural by taping three strips of bulletin board paper together: blue for water, green for land, and light blue for air. Label each section accordingly. When a child visits the center, have him use the art supplies to create any type of transportation. When each child's project is ready, help him glue it to the appropriate section of the mural.

Discovery Center

▶ *experimentation*
▶ *critical thinking*
▶ *observation skills*
▶ *making comparisons*
▶ *drawing conclusions*

Way to Go!

Scientific minds are all geared up for thinking with this activity. To prepare, stock a center with a supply of toy vehicles such as cars, boats, planes, and trucks. Also provide a wide board, blocks, and sheets of various textured items such as bubble wrap, waxed paper, and sandpaper. Encourage children who visit this center to use the board and the blocks to create a ramp. Invite them to send the vehicles down the ramp and observe what happens. Then encourage them to try the same thing with sandpaper (for example) on the ramp. What happens? Invite them to change the angle of the ramp and use the other textured sheets to make all kinds of discoveries. So what's the fastest way to go? The slowest?

Alphabet Train

All aboard for alphabetical-order practice! To prepare cut out a construction paper copy of the train engine pattern on page 35 as well as 26 boxcar shapes. (Also cut out two black construction paper wheels to glue on each boxcar.) Write a different letter on each boxcar. To do this activity, have a child position the engine on the left side of his workspace. Then encourage him to line up the rest of the cars in alphabetical order.

Literacy Center

letter recognition ◄
sequencing ◄

Number Train

This train is on track for numeration skills! In advance, cut out a copy of the train engine pattern on page 35 as well as ten simple boxcar shapes. Also cut out two light gray wheels for each boxcar. Use a marker to write a different number word on each boxcar. For each number word, program one wheel with the corresponding number and one wheel with the corresponding dot set. To do this activity, have a child position the train engine on the left side of her workspace. Then encourage her to arrange the boxcars in numerical order behind the engine. Finally, ask her to match each corresponding wheel to its boxcar.

Math Center

number recognition ◄
counting ◄

33

- *fine motor*
- *creative thinking*
- *problem solving*

Building Bridges

Invite your youngsters to build these bridges to all sorts of learning! To prepare, make a land-river workmat by gluing a blue construction paper river across a green sheet of construction paper. Then laminate the workmat. Put the workmat in a center along with a supply of play dough, craft sticks, small toy cars, people, or farm animals. When a child visits this center, encourage him to use the supplies to build a bridge across the river. When the bridge is completed, invite him to try crossing it with the cars, people, or farm animals.

Work Crew

The crew is working hard—and learning a lot—at this center. In advance, design special "work orders" based on the types of blocks you have in your classroom. (See the examples below.) Also provide hard hats and large toy dump trucks. When a child visits this center, have him pick up a work order and then take a dump truck to the blocks to fill the order. Next, have him deliver the order to a designated work site. When all of the orders are filled, invite the crew members to build a creation with the supplies.

- *role-playing*
- *number recognition*
- *counting*

TEC61183

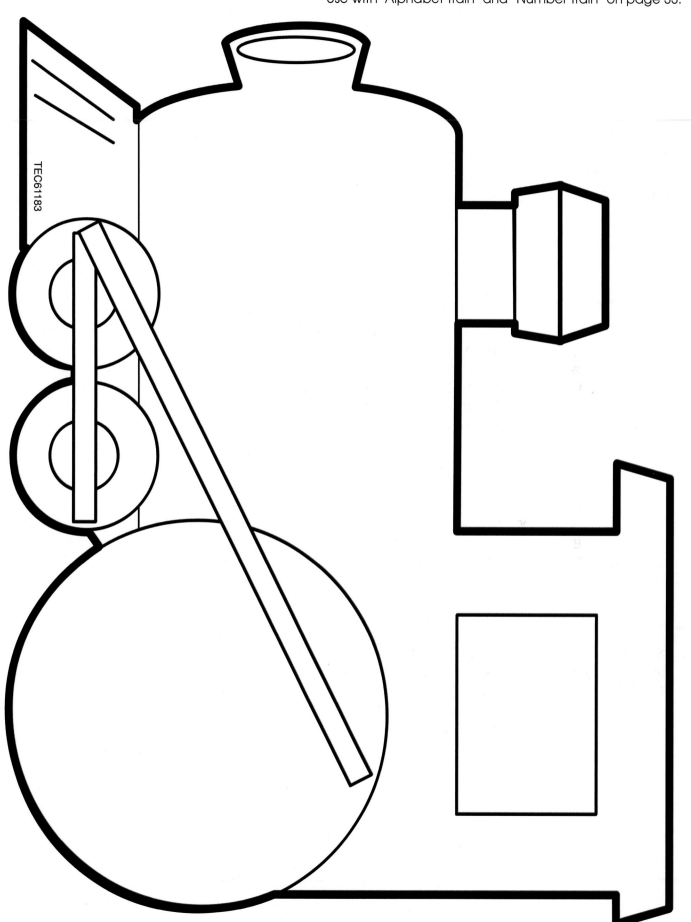

Gingerbread Junction

Goodness gracious—it's gingerbread time! Serve up these sweet centers for lots of learning fun.

Literacy Center

▶ story retelling
▶ book knowledge and appreciation
▶ oral language

Gingerbread Storytelling

Your students will run, run, run as fast as they can to this story re-telling center! In advance, spread a coat of glue all over the bowl of a plastic spoon; then sprinkle ginger and cinnamon on it. When the glue is dry, put the spoon in a basket along with a small bowl, a gingerbread man cookie cutter, artificial greenery, and wooden blocks. Cover a table with a decorative tablecloth and place the filled basket and a cookie sheet under the table. After sharing your favorite versions of *The Gingerbread Man,* display the books on the table. Invite students to explore the book selections and use the props to retell the story.

Math Center

▶ reproducing shapes
▶ spatial awareness
▶ fine motor

Sh-Sh-Shape It!

In advance, duplicate the shape cards (page 39) onto construction paper. Color, cut out, and laminate the cards. Store the cards in a recipe box. Place the recipe box in a center along with a class supply of napkins and gumdrop-shaped cutouts. When a child visits the center, have her take a napkin to use as her workspace. Then ask her to choose a shape card from the box. Encourage her to use the gumdrop cutouts to reproduce that shape on her napkin. Then have her clear off her napkin and choose another shape card. Invite her to repeat the activity until she has made each shape. Look! A gumdrop triangle!

The Cookie Jar

This particular cookie jar provides fine-motor practice with the scent of ginger and a side order of math skills, too! In advance, fill a plastic jar with large gingersnaps. Place the jar in a center along with a pair of tongs, a medium-sized cookie sheet, a pencil, and scrap paper. Invite each child to estimate the number of cookies it will take to cover the sheet. After he writes down his guess, have him use the tongs to place the cookies side by side on the sheet. When the cookie sheet is covered, have the child count the number of gingersnaps used and compare it to his guess.

Motor Center

fine motor ◄
estimation ◄
counting ◄
comparing ◄

Cottage Creations

Spice up your sensory center with this cottage-making idea! In advance, prepare a batch of Gingerbread Play Dough. Put the play dough in your sensory center along with a rolling pin, cookie cutters, assorted holiday-related craft foam cutouts, and sequins. When a child visits the center, encourage him to use the supplies to make a pretend gingerbread cottage. (Although this dough smells mighty nice, it's just for hands-on fun!)

Sensory Center

creative ◄
expression
fine motor ◄
spatial awareness ◄

Gingerbread Play Dough

Ingredients:
1½ c. all-purpose flour
1 c. salt
1 tbsp. powdered alum
1 tbsp. vegetable oil
1 c. boiling water
brown paste food coloring
1 tbsp. pumpkin pie spice

Directions:
In a large bowl, combine the flour, salt, and alum. Add the oil and boiling water; then stir until well blended. Add the spice and coloring; then knead the dough until it is smooth. Store the dough in an airtight container.

Home, *Sweet* Home

Tempt your students' imaginations with this dramatic-play center. In advance, make a cottage by using a craft knife to cut a door and two window openings in a large brown appliance box. Next, refer to the ideas below to make pretend candies. Attach a Velcro® dot to the back of each candy piece. Then attach the corresponding Velcro dots to the cottage. Arrange the cottage and candies in a center along with wooden blocks. When students visit the center, invite them to decorate the cottage and use the blocks to make a gingerbread path. Knock, knock!

Dramatic-Play Center

▶ creative thinking
▶ role-playing

Gumdrop
Paint a foam ball half with a mixture of one part glue and two parts tempera paint. Sprinkle clear glitter on top of the paint; then set it aside to dry.

Lollipop
Tape a large craft stick to the flat side of a plastic lid. On the opposite side, use a permanent marker to make designs.

Peppermint Stick
Tape the ends of two lengths of red yarn to the top inside of a white cardboard tube. Wrap the yarn around the tube to resemble stripes. Then tape the other ends to the bottom inside of the tube. (Striped straws can also be used to resemble smaller peppermint sticks.)

Peppermint Disc
Use a marker to draw swirls on any size foam ball. Wrap the ball with clear plastic wrap; then tie each end with a length of yarn.

Ginger Candy

This gingery treat is sure to stir up your youngsters' senses! In advance, mix up a batch of candy dough (see the recipe below). Sandwich the dough between two sheets of waxed paper; then place it in your cooking center. Also provide a supply of napkins and a plastic knife. Invite each center visitor to knead the dough through the waxed paper. Then have her lift the top layer of waxed paper and cut off a small portion of dough (about the size of a quarter). After she rolls her dough into a ball, have her shape it to resemble a gumdrop. Ready to eat!

Cooking Center

▶ following directions
▶ fine motor
▶ sensory experience

Ingredients:
one 3-oz. package of cream cheese, softened
3 c. powdered sugar

1 tbsp. cinnamon
½ tsp. ground ginger

Directions:
1. Mix the cream cheese, cinnamon, and ground ginger in a bowl. Add a cup of powdered sugar at a time and mix until a dough forms.
2. Knead the dough thoroughly, adding extra powdered sugar if the dough becomes sticky.

TEC61183

TEC61183

TEC61183

TEC61183

TEC61183

TEC61183

Shapin' Up!

Circles and triangles and squares—oh my!
Give these shapely centers a try!

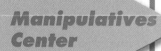

Manipulatives Center

▶ sorting
▶ visual discrimination
▶ matching

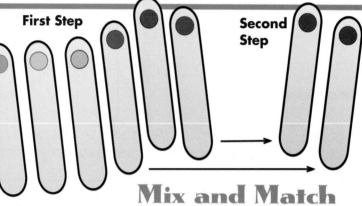

First Step   **Second Step**

Mix and Match

Matching and sorting skills shape right up with this idea! To prepare, use colored markers to program pairs of large craft sticks with matching shapes of the same color. Invite youngsters to first sort the sticks by shape. Then have them further sort the shapes by color until they match all the pairs. For an added challenge, program sets of sticks with two or three shapes on each one; then encourage youngsters to find the matching patterns. So simple. So fun!

Literacy Center

▶ shape identification
▶ word recognition
▶ left-to-right progression
▶ fine motor

△ triangle

○ circle

Read It, Write It

Watch those literacy skills take shape before your very eyes! To prepare, draw a different shape on each of a supply of sentence strips. Next to each shape, write its name in large letters. Laminate the strips; then place them in your literacy center along with wipe-off markers and a dry-erase eraser. When a child visits the center, have her identify the shape and read the word on each sentence strip and then use the marker to trace over the shape and the word. Cleanup takes only a wipe of the eraser!

Shape Bags

The preparation for *this* discovery center goes to your students! Give each child a paper lunch bag and ask him to draw a shape on one panel. Then have him take the bag home and find something that is the same shape. As the shape bags come back to school, have each child place his object in your discovery center. Then encourage youngsters to take a closer look to see how many shapes they can discover. Hey—a rectangle scarf!

Water Wonders

Shapes in the water table? Sure! Why not? To prepare, cut out a variety of shapes from craft foam. Use a permanent marker to trace each shape onto a foam tray. Scatter the shapes in the water and stack the programmed trays nearby. When a child visits this center, have her float the trays on the water. Then encourage her to search the water to find a shape to match each corresponding outline on the trays.

Magic Act

You won't need magic words to see the trick at this center! Use chalk to draw shapes near the bottom of a chalkboard. (If you have only individual lap chalkboards, draw shapes on each one of those instead.) Provide large paintbrushes (or small paintbrushes for lap boards) and water. Invite children to use the brushes and water to paint over the shapes. Surprise! The shapes disappear!

Block Shapes

Continue to work with shapes in your block center! On the floor of your block area, use colored tape to create large outlines of different shapes. For this activity, have a child select a type of block to arrange along the outline of a shape. How many blocks will it take to cover the tape? Will there be enough blocks? What will she do if she runs out of blocks? What a fun way to review shapes and build problem-solving skills!

Sing a Song of Shapes

Is that the sound of music you hear? Absolutely! For each shape that you're studying, cut out two or three large construction paper samples; then laminate them. Store the shapes in a string-tie envelope. Then make a tape recording of the song below, substituting a different shape each time you repeat the verse. Place the shapes in a center along with the tape and a tape player. Invite one to three children at a time to listen to the song and manipulate the shape cutouts according to the song. Tune in to shapes!

Music and Movement Center

listening skills ◄
following directions ◄
shape recognition ◄

If You Have a Circle
(sung to the tune of "Did You Ever See a Lassie?")

Oh, if you have a (circle), a (circle), a (circle),
Oh, if you have a (circle), then hold it up high!
Wave it this way and that way,
Then that way and this way.
Oh, if you have a (circle), then hold it up high!

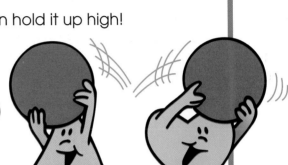

The Shape of Art

Shapes galore create art and more! Cut a supply of geometric shapes from light-colored construction paper. Then put the shapes in a center along with crayons, markers, glue, art paper, and assorted art supplies. Have each youngster choose one or more shapes to transform into a picture. Will the circle become a smiley face? A snowball? A big, bright sun? Just shape it up to see!

Art Center

shape ◄
discrimination
creative ◄
expression
spatial awareness ◄

Penguin Pals

Pal up with penguins for lots of playful learning at these curriculum-friendly centers.

Math Center

▶ *size discrimination*
▶ *numeral sequencing*

Everybody, Line Up!

Practice size seriation with these penguin pals. First, color and cut out a copy of the penguin family on page 47. Glue each penguin to a different foam cup as shown. Using a permanent marker, label the back rim of each cup with a numeral from 1 to 5 to show the size order of the penguins *from smallest to largest.* To do this activity, ask a child to arrange the penguins in a line from smallest to largest. To check her work, have the child check (or ask you to check) the numeral sequence on the cups. For an added challenge, have a child stack the cups by penguin size, beginning with the *largest* penguin on the bottom.

Fancy Penguins

Plenty of color-word practice awaits your youngsters when they dress these penguins in style! For each color that you'd like to include, copy the penguin and bow tie patterns (page 47) on white construction paper. Write a different color word on the belly of each penguin and color a bow tie to match; then color and cut out the penguins. To do this activity, have a child match each bow tie to the penguin with the corresponding color word. All dressed up!

Literacy Center

▶ *color words*
▶ *color recognition*

44

Ready, Set, Slide!

Slip and slide into measurement skills with these playful penguins! To make one penguin, copy the smallest pattern from the penguin family on page 47. Then fill an empty black film canister with sand and snap on the lid. Next, glue the penguin pattern to the canister. Place all the penguins in an uncarpeted area of your room, along with a supply of unlined index cards (icebergs). Use masking tape to designate a starting line. When a child visits this center, have her kneel at the starting line and slide a penguin across the floor. Then ask her to use the icebergs to measure the distance. How many icebergs? Invite the child to repeat the penguin slide again and compare the distances. Whee!

Discovery Center

measurement ◀
counting ◀

Swim, Penguins, Swim!

Dive right in and experience this very unique version of surf and sea. To prepare, use a fine-tip permanent marker to draw a simple penguin on each of a supply of Ping-Pong® balls. Fill a sensory tub with rice (tinted blue if you like!); then bury the penguins in it. When a child visits the center, have him comb through the "waters" with his hands to catch the swimming penguins. If desired, post a specified number of penguins to find each day and challenge students to find exactly that many. Swim, penguins, swim!

Sensory Center

tactile experience ◀
fine motor ◀

Perky Little Penguins

These magnets make great math manipulatives for school or adorable refrigerator pals for home. To prepare, make tracers by cutting out tagboard copies of the penguin body on page 47. Place these tracers in a center along with wooden craft spoons, black craft foam, orange construction paper scraps, craft glue, and blue pens. To make a penguin, use the pen to trace the penguin body pattern onto the black craft foam; then cut it out. (For younger children, provide precut foam shapes.) Glue a craft spoon onto the black cutout to resemble the penguin's head and body. Use a black marker to draw eyes, and then glue on an orange construction paper beak and feet. To complete the penguin, attach a strip of magnetic tape to the back. Hello, little pal!

Penguin Playground

Invite little ones to use their imaginations to create a pretend romp for penguins. Gather a supply of white foam packaging pieces and peanuts. In preparation, make several penguins as described in "Ready, Set, Slide!" on page 45. Place the penguins and white supplies in your block center. Then invite children to invent a playground for penguins. Before you know it, you'll have banks, icebergs, and even sloping hills. Penguins, get ready to waddle, slide, dive, and glide!

penguin family
Use with "Everybody, Line Up!" on page 44 and use the
smallest penguin with "Ready, Set, Slide!" on page 45.

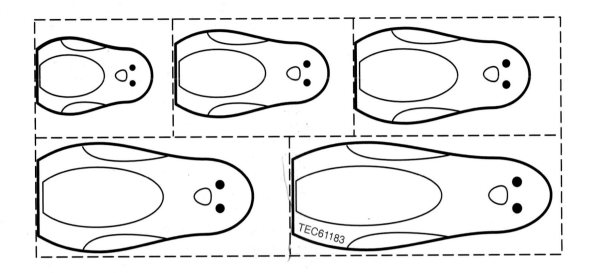

bow tie and penguin
Use with "Fancy Penguins" on page 44.

penguin body
Use with "Perky Little Penguins" on page 46.

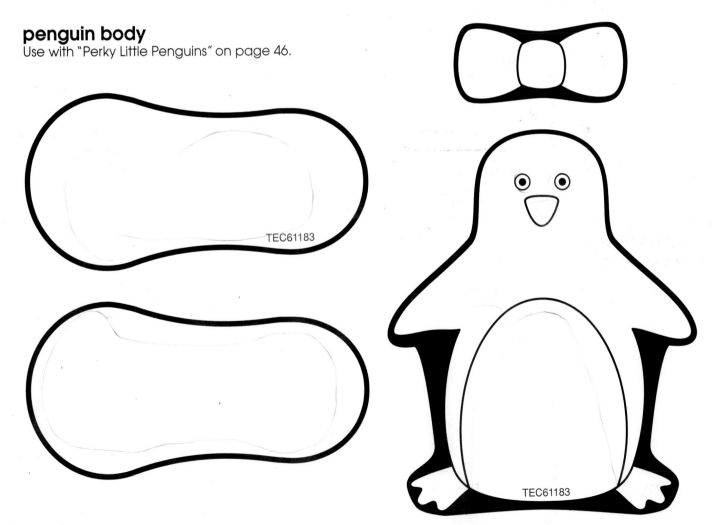

TEC61183

Marvelous Mittens

Want to keep your youngsters' skills warmed up? Create the perfect learning climate with these mitten-inspired centers!

Literacy Center

▶ name recognition

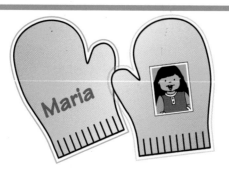

Mitten Match

Whose mittens are these? Your youngsters will find out with this reading activity. In advance, duplicate the pair of mittens on page 51 onto various colors of construction paper to make a class supply. For each child, cut out a pair of same-colored mittens. Program one mitten with the child's name; then glue that child's photo on the matching mitten. Laminate all the cutouts; then place them in a center. When a child visits this center, have him read the name on a mitten and then pair it with the corresponding photo on another mitten. For older children, program mittens with first and last names. Hey, Zachary! I found your mittens!

Which Is Warmer?

In your discovery center, provide several different types of mittens, including a waterproof pair. Place a bucket of snow (or ice cubes) in the center; then invite youngsters to dig in! Instruct each child to explore the snow using the different types of mittens and discuss her discoveries. It won't take long to discover that dry mittens are warm mittens!

Discovery Center

▶ sensory experience
▶ making comparisons
▶ drawing conclusions

Lacing Mittens

Give little hands big fine-motor practice with these sturdy lacing mittens. To make them, use a permanent marker to trace the outline of the mitten patterns (page 51) onto colorful plastic placemats and then cut them out. Hole-punch around the perimeter of each mitten. Place the mittens in a center along with plastic needles and a supply of brightly colored laces. (For younger children, thread each needle; then tie the end of the yarn around one of the holes at the bottom of a mitten cutout.) Invite youngsters to lace around the mittens.

Motor Center

fine motor ◀
patterning ◀
hand-eye ◀
coordination

Mittens and More

If your children enjoy activities using the popular "feely box" idea, try this sensory table twist. In advance, gather several different pairs of mittens and put them in a pillowcase. Invite a child to reach inside the pillowcase and pull out one mitten. Then have him reach in the pillowcase again and try to find that mitten's match without looking. Encourage the child to repeat the activity until all the mittens have been matched.

Sensory Center

sorting ◀
tactile ◀
discrimination
matching ◀

▶ fine motor
▶ sorting
▶ creative thinking

Mitten Clip

The mitten laundry is now open! Stock a laundry basket with a variety of mittens. Place the laundry basket in your dramatic-play area along with a supply of clothespins. Then make a clothesline by stringing a length of rope between two chairs. When a child visits this center, have him clip the mittens onto the clothesline. Encourage him to be creative as he thinks of different ways to sort and arrange the mittens.

▶ visual
  discrimination
▶ patterning

Mitten Patterns

These festive mittens are a perfect match for a patterning center! Make mitten tracers from the patterns on page 51. Trace a large supply of mitten shapes onto different types of craft paper; then cut them out. Laminate all the cutouts; then place them in your math center. Have youngsters who visit the center use the mittens to make patterns.

Mitten Patterns

Use with "Mitten Match" on page 48, "Lacing Mittens" on page 49, and "Mitten Patterns" on page 50.

TEC61183

Dinosaur Days!

These center ideas are sure to have your little ones thundering around with enthusiasm for those reptiles from long, long ago!

Discovery Center

▶ investigating size
▶ measurement
▶ problem solving

Dino Feet Can't Be Beat!

This activity is sure to have an enormous impact on how your little learners view the size of dinosaur feet! To prepare, use bulletin board paper to make a large footprint similar to the one shown. Next, invite youngsters to take off their shoes. Encourage them to arrange the shoes in a variety of ways to discover just how many shoes fit on the large dinosaur footprint. Stomp, stomp!

Art Center

▶ fine motor
▶ following directions

Prehistoric Puppets

These baby dinosaur puppets are sure to fill your room with bouncing bundles of prehistoric fun! Make a class supply of page 55 on green construction paper. Then fold one nine-inch paper plate in half for each child. Place these items at a center along with scissors, glue sticks, markers, and a completed sample. Direct each child to color a plate and then cut out the pattern pieces. Have him glue the pieces on his plate as shown. Then help him punch two holes in the rounded part of the plate as shown. Tie one end of each of two lengths of yarn through each hole and then tie the opposite ends around a craft stick. These dinosaurs are ready to dance!

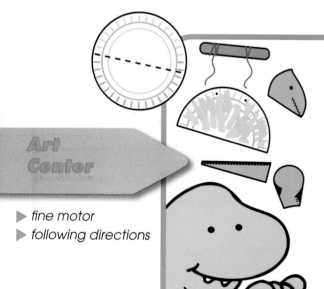

The Great Dinosaur Exploration!

Give your junior scientists a feel for what it was like to live in the time of the dinosaurs! To prepare the center, cover a small table with a blanket (cave), place a blue paper oval on the floor (pond), and stack several pillows (mountain or volcano). Put plastic dinosaurs, backpacks, maps, toy binoculars, and different-sized plastic eggs at the center. Encourage students to use their baby dinosaurs from "Prehistoric Puppets" on page 52 as they explore their surroundings. In no time, you're sure to have dinosaurs crawling, climbing, and stomping through the swamp. Roarrr!

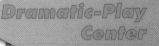
Dramatic-Play Center

role-playing ◄
creative thinking ◄

Story Swamp

Rev up your students' interest in this swampy atmosphere filled with dinosaur tales! Fill an inflated swimming pool with shredded newspaper. Then hide dinosaur books beneath the swampy grasses. It won't take long before your ferociously friendly dinosaur lovers climb in and read!

Literacy Center

book knowledge ◄
and appreciation

▶ sensory experience
▶ exploration and
  discovery
▶ fine motor

Those Amazing Bones!

Your little archaeologists are sure to dig right into this "dino-mite" sand table! Bury items such as plastic bones, rocks, shells, and bark. For added fun, place a scale, magnifying glasses, rulers, clean paintbrushes (for dusting off finds), sieves, small plastic shovels, clipboards, paper, and pencils near the table. Then invite your young explorers to search for prehistoric items. No bones about it, digging is fun!

▶ matching shapes

In Shape With Dinosaurs

Youngsters' imaginations will run wild when they create these shapely dinosaurs! In advance, make dinosaur mats similar to the ones shown by tracing different tagboard shapes onto sheets of construction paper. Place the mats at a center along with construction paper shapes (cut to match the mats). A child selects a mat and then matches the manipulatives to the corresponding shapes on her mat. For added fun, encourage youngsters to use the manipulatives to make their own prehistoric creatures!

legs

head

tail

TEC61183

TERRIFIC TEETH

Use these dental-health centers to brush up on cross-curricular skills!

Toothy Grins

This center activity will bring miles of tooth-bearing smiles. For each number that you'd like to include in this center, duplicate the mouth pattern (page 59) on red construction paper. Cut out each pattern; then mount it on a poster board card. Program each card with a numeral or number word; then laminate the cards. Store all the cards and a bag of miniature marshmallows in a large resealable bag. For this activity, a child arranges all the mouth cards on a flat surface. Then he places the appropriate number of marshmallow teeth inside each mouth. Grin and count it!

Math Center

▶ counting
▶ number and/or number-word recognition
▶ fine motor

Pearly Whites

These pearly whites have personality! For each child, enlarge and copy a tooth pattern (page 59) on white construction paper. Place the patterns in a center along with crayons, markers, scissors, glue, craft sticks, and various art supplies. When a child visits this center, invite her to transform a tooth cutout into a tooth puppet by adding clothing, hair, and facial features. Then have her glue a craft stick to the back of her puppet. During a group time, have each child use her puppet as she sings the song in the music and movement center (page 58).

Art Center

▶ creative expression
▶ fine motor

Toothpaste Box Puzzles

Kids love puzzles! And they'll love the unique twist of using recycled toothpaste boxes. In advance, ask parents to send in empty toothpaste boxes in a variety of brands. To make one puzzle, use a craft knife to puzzle-cut the box into three sections. Tape the ends with clear tape; then tape crumpled paper inside each piece so that the box retains its three-dimensional shape. Place all the pieces in a basket in your center. For this activity, encourage a child to find three puzzle pieces that go together. Then have her arrange the pieces so that they reveal a kind of toothpaste. Look! It's Sparkle!

Manipulatives Center

fine motor ◄
visual discrimination ◄
print awareness ◄

I'm in Advertising Now!

Smile and put your best jingle forward! Stock a center with a supply of white construction paper, crayons, markers, scissors, old magazines, and glue. For this activity, ask each child to think of a new kind of toothpaste. Encourage her to design an ad for her original product by using the supplies to illustrate and write or dictate about it. During a group time, have each child share her ad with the class. Afterward, bind all the pages together to make a class book of newly invented toothpastes.

Literacy Center

creative thinking ◄
creative writing ◄
fine motor ◄

Dental Discoveries

To set up this center, position a mirror at child height. Also provide a supply of paper, crayons, and pencils. Before opening this center, prompt children with questions such as the following: What color are your teeth? How many teeth do you have? Are any of your teeth missing or loose? What keeps your teeth in your mouth? Instruct each child to wash his hands before taking a turn in the center. Then have him take a peek in the mirror at his own teeth to see what he can find out! Encourage children to write about and illustrate their discoveries.

Discovery Center

▶ observation skills
▶ counting
▶ recording information

Brushing Melody

Invite your students to use the puppets they have made in the art center (page 56) as they sing the song below. These pearly whites have something to sing about!

Music and Movement Center

▶ participating in a song
▶ creative expression

Take Care of Us!
(sung to the tune of "Row, Row, Row Your Boat")

Brush, brush, brush us, please.
Brush us every day.
Brush, brush, brush us, please,
To fight that tooth decay!

Rinse, rinse, rinse us, please.
Rinse us every day.
Rinse, rinse, rinse us, please,
To fight that tooth decay!

Eat, eat, eat good foods
To keep us mighty strong.
Eat, eat, eat good foods,
And we'll last very long!

Mouth Pattern
Use with "Toothy Grins" on page 56.

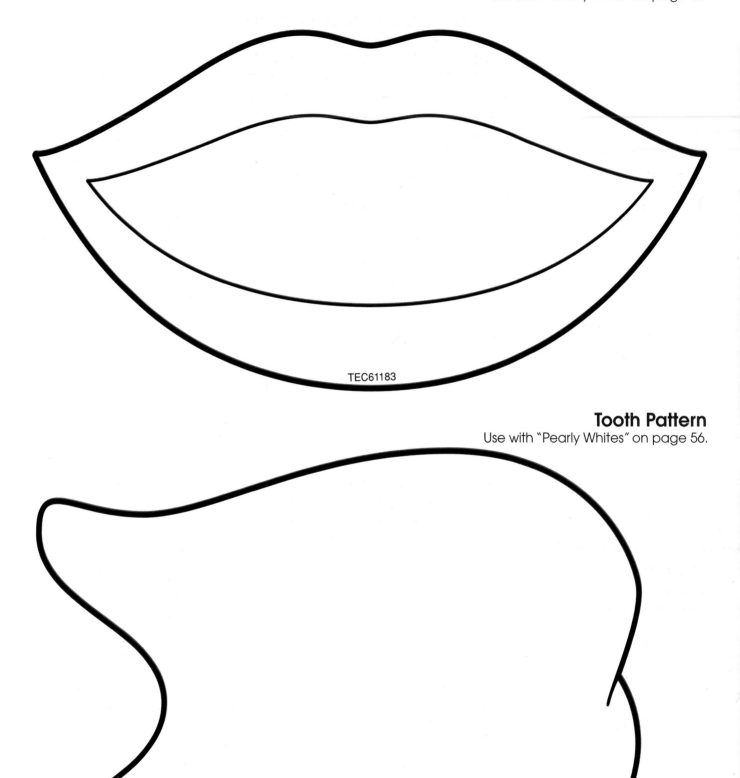

TEC61183

Tooth Pattern
Use with "Pearly Whites" on page 56.

TEC61183

SWEET HEARTS

Sweeten youngsters' appetite for learning with these heart-related center ideas!

Math Center

▶ *counting*
▶ *measurement*
▶ *estimation*

Counting Hearts

Math skills beat right along with this "heart-y" center idea. To prepare, stock a center with a few empty heart-shaped boxes, small gift boxes, and a container of small craft foam hearts. Encourage children to create different ways to arrange the hearts inside the boxes. How many hearts does it take to go *around* the shape of each box? To go *across* each box? To divide each box right down the middle? If desired, keep a supply of Valentine's Day stickers available to reward a job well done!

Sensory Center

▶ *fine motor*
▶ *tactile experience*
▶ *observation skills*

Hearts So Full

Here's an idea that's soaked with learning opportunities! In advance, cut out a supply of heart shapes from a variety of craft sponges. Sprinkle heart-shaped confetti in your water table and, if desired, use red food coloring to tint the water. Place the dry sponges near the water along with some bowls and cups. As little ones visit this center, invite them to observe what happens when they dunk the sponges in the water. Also prompt children to see how much water they can squeeze out of the water-soaked sponges.

Friendship Bracelets

This lovely piece of jewelry might look like a simple bracelet, but you'll know it's a creative tool for reinforcing friendships and fine-motor skills. Provide a supply of pipe cleaners along with a large supply of uncooked macaroni tinted red, and craft foam hearts, each with a hole punched in the center. When a child visits this center, have him choose a pipe cleaner and then string on his selection of macaroni and hearts in the pattern of his choice. Have him twist the ends together to make a bracelet sized to slip over his hand. When everyone has made a bracelet, encourage each child to trade bracelets with a classmate. From my heart to yours!

Motor Center

fine motor ◀
patterning ◀
socialization ◀

Disappearing Hearts

What happens to candy hearts when they are immersed in warm water? How about ice water? Or just left out in the air? Invite your youngsters to help you investigate and find out the answers! Stock the center with a supply of candy conversation hearts, clear plastic cups, craft sticks (for stirring), and a bowl of ice. Before opening this center, prompt students to make predictions by asking the questions mentioned above. Next, have a child put an ice cube in a cup. Then have her fill the cup with cold water and fill another cup with warm water. Encourage children to use the supplies to find out what happens to candy hearts left in the different places. Any ideas *why*?

Discovery Center

observation ◀
prediction ◀
experimentation ◀

Here's a Heart!

Your students will definitely deliver when it comes to passing along these heartfelt sentiments. In advance, stock a center with a variety of valentines or construction paper heart cutouts. Also provide markers, stickers, envelopes, a class list, and a mailbox (or decorated box). Encourage children visiting this center to write or dictate valentines to their classmates and then deposit them in the mailbox. At the end of center time, empty the mailbox and deliver the hearty greetings!

Literacy Center

▶ fine motor
▶ writing skills
▶ socialization

Heart Art

Children will be delighted to make these fancy hearts all by themselves! In advance, collect different sizes of empty thread spools. For each child, duplicate the heart pattern (page 63) on red or pink construction paper. Arrange the heart patterns and spools in a center along with white tempera paint, paintbrushes, and slightly damp sponges. Provide sheets of red, pink, or white construction paper, scissors, and glue for the backing. Instruct a child to paint a thin coat of white paint onto a sponge. Then have her use the painted sponge as a stamp pad, pressing one end of a spool into the sponge and then onto the heart cutout as desired. When the paint is dry, have each child cut out her heart and then mount it on a sheet of construction paper.

Art Center

▶ fine motor
▶ creative expression
▶ spatial awareness

TEC61183

It's Nursery Rhyme Time!

Your little ones are headed for a treasury of cross-curricular learning fun when they visit these centers highlighting some of their favorite rhymes.

Math Center

▶ *counting*
▶ *spatial awareness*
▶ *gross motor*

Jumping Jacks and Jills!

Just how nimble and quick are your students? Find out with a roll of the die! To make a die, cover a cube-shaped tissue box with colorful paper or an adhesive covering. Use sticky dots or a permanent marker to program the dots on the die. Place the die in the center along with six large laminated candle cutouts. When a child visits this center, instruct her to arrange the candles each about two feet apart in a row. Then have her roll the die, count the dots, and jump over that many candles (one at a time). For an added challenge, have the child roll the die, count the dots, and arrange that many candles side by side. Then have her try to jump over the group of candles all at once! Jack and Jill be nimble!

Rub-a-dub-dub

Rub-a-dub-dub, how many in a tub? That's what your classroom crew will find out when they make active learning discoveries at this water-filled table. First, gather a supply of small waterproof toy people and animal figures and a variety of empty food tubs. Arrange the supplies near your water table. When youngsters visit this center, encourage them to fill the tubs with varying numbers of toy people and animals. How many people fit inside any given tub before it starts to tip? Will the tub sink completely? Does each tub hold the same number of people? It's rub-a-dub-dub discovery fun!

Sensory Center

▶ *experimentation*
▶ *observation*
▶ *critical thinking*
▶ *counting*

Discovery Center

observation skills ◄
experimenting with ◄
inclined planes
making comparisons ◄

Down the Hill!

Oops! Jack and Jill *tumbled* down the hill, but your youngsters will make lots of discoveries as they help toy cars *roll* down this hill. To prepare, create a ramp (hill) by placing a smooth piece of wood on a stack of blocks from your block center. When a child visits this center, have her position a toy car at the top of the ramp and then let go and watch it roll down. How far did the car roll? Encourage the child to change the height of the ramp and then repeat the roll. Did the car roll further when the ramp was higher or lower? How about another car? Same or different results?

London Bridges

Youngsters cruise into creativity as they construct numerous bridges and then *help* the bridges fall! In advance, cut a length of blue bulletin board paper to resemble a river; then tape it to the floor in your block area. When children visit this center, encourage them to sing a few rounds of "London Bridge" as they cooperatively build and rebuild bridges across the river. Get ready! London Bridge is about to fall down!

Block Center

problem solving ◄
creative thinking ◄
spatial awareness ◄

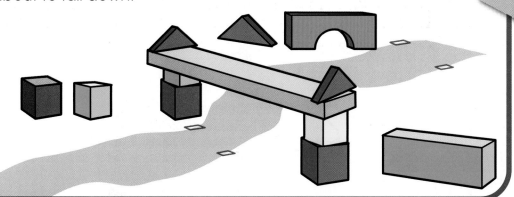

Literacy Center

- *oral language*
- *print awareness*
- *writing skills*

Mark It With a *B!*

Students bake up a big batch of language skills when they create these special letter cakes. In advance, stock the center with play dough, a rolling pin, plastic knives, spatulas, foam trays (to use as cookie sheets), and a shoebox (to use as an oven). Write the "Pat-a-Cake" nursery rhyme on chart paper; then display it in the center. Encourage each baker to read/recite the rhyme as he rolls out the dough. Then have him cut out a cake. Next, have him use the knife to mark it with a *B* and then slide it onto a tray and into the oven. To extend this activity, encourage each child to create a cake for each letter of his name. Bake me some letter cakes as fast as you can!

Pat-a-Cake
Pat-a-cake, pat-a-cake, baker's man.
Bake me a cake as fast as you can.
Roll it, and pat it, and mark it with a *B*.
Then put it in the oven for baby and me!

Cooking Center

- *eye-hand coordination*
- *measurement*
- *following directions*

Mary's Sure-to-Go Snacks

Your students will flock to this center to make these tempting snacks. In advance, copy, color, and cut out the recipe cards on page 67. Display the cards in sequence in your cooking area. When a child visits this center, invite him to follow the directions to make a snack for himself. This great snack is sure to go with each of your little lambs!

Mary's Sure-to-Go Snacks

Ingredients for each child:
¼ c. mini pretzel twists
fish-shaped crackers
O-shaped cereal
animal crackers

Utensils and supplies:
one zippered plastic bag per child
¼ c. measuring cup
1 tbsp. measuring spoon

Teacher preparation:
Arrange the ingredients and supplies for easy student access.

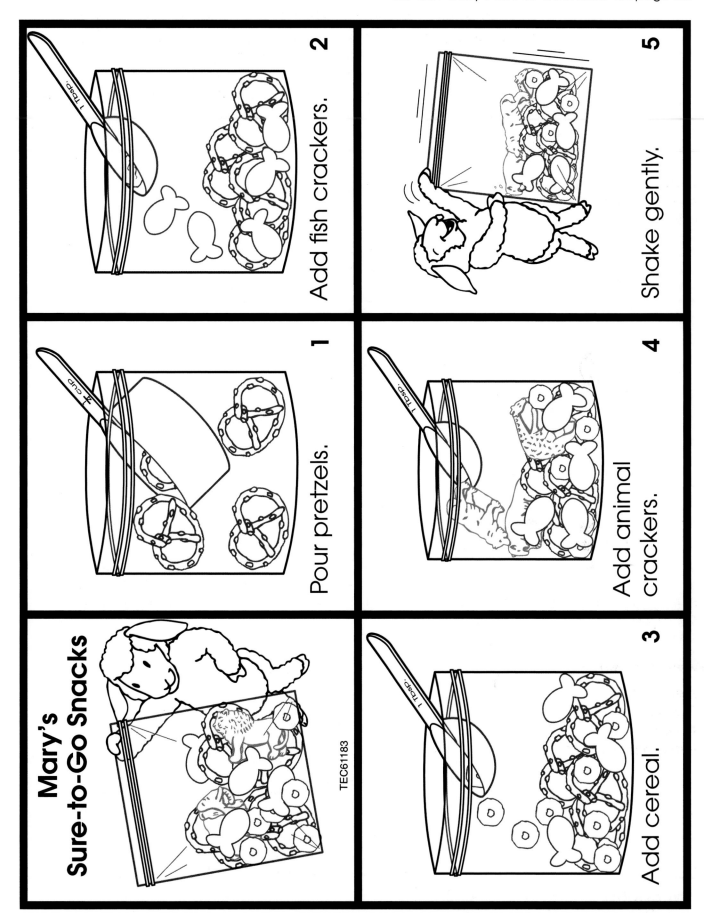

2 Add fish crackers.

1 Pour pretzels.

Mary's Sure-to-Go Snacks

TEC61183

5 Shake gently.

4 Add animal crackers.

3 Add cereal.

Beggin' for Eggs

These springtime centers scramble eggs with lots of learning. So let's get crackin'!

Math Center

▶ *creating patterns*
▶ *copying patterns*
▶ *color matching*

A Patterned Dozen

Pair up students at the math center for some patterning practice. Cut the lid off a clean, sanitized egg carton. Fill the lid with plastic eggs (in solid colors). Place the top and bottom of the carton on a tabletop.

To complete the activity, use the eggs to create a pattern in the top row of egg cups. Next, the child copies the pattern in the bottom row of cups. If desired, tape the egg-cup portions from two cartons together to create longer rows for more complex patterns. "Egg-cellent"!

Humpty Dumpties

All the king's horses and all the king's men are needed to put *these* eggs back together again! To prepare, gather 12 plastic eggs, a basket, and an empty egg carton cleaned and sanitized. Use a permanent marker to label the halves of each egg with a matching uppercase and lowercase letter. (For younger students, use egg halves of the same color. For older students, mix up the egg colors.) Now separate the eggs and place the pieces in the basket.

Direct the child visiting this center to unscramble the pieces and put the eggs together by matching the letters. Instruct her to place the whole eggs in the carton. If desired, pick 12 sequential letters to work on and label each egg cup in the carton with one of these different letters. Then have the child put the completed eggs in order according to the labeled cups. Check each student's work and reward her efforts with an Easter egg sticker. A, B, C, D, E-gg!

Literacy Center

▶ *uppercase and lowercase letter matching*
▶ *letter sequence*

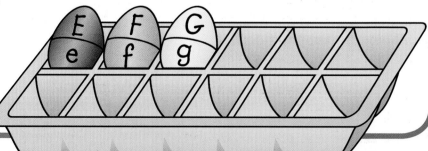

Egg Layers

Keep your youngsters guessing with this eggy game. To prepare, draw a simple gameboard on tagboard, similar to the one shown. Make a copy of the cards on page 71. Color the cards and then cut them apart on the dotted lines. Fold each card in half and tape the ends together. If desired, laminate the cards and gameboard.

To play the game, stack the cards with the animal sides faceup on the board. Give each of two players a game piece, such as a bingo chip or a seasonal counter. Have the first player identify the animal on top of the stack and guess whether it lays eggs. Then instruct the child to turn the card over to check his guess. If he is correct, he moves his game piece one space. If he is incorrect, play continues with the next player and the next card. Once all the cards are used, shuffle them and stack them faceup again. The game ends when one (or both) players reach the finish line.

Literacy Center

critical thinking ◄
number ◄
sequence
taking turns ◄

How Do You Like 'Em?

Your sensory center is the perfect place for this egg-tasting graph. Arrange to have parent volunteers work with small groups of students to prepare two or three different egg dishes, such as deviled eggs, scrambled eggs, omelettes, quiche, French toast, or egg salad. Make a grid containing the names of the prepared foods. Have each child sample the foods and then color a block on the grid to indicate her favorite egg choice. Now it's time to "eggs-amine" the graph's results!

Sensory Center

exploring taste ◄
graphing ◄

How Do You Like 'Em?		
Deviled	Scrambled	French Toast

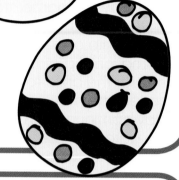

Art Center

▶ fine motor
▶ creative expression

Expressive Eggs

These unique keepsakes will turn givers' *and* receivers' faces sunny-side up. To prepare, write the verse shown on a tagboard egg shape for each child. Have each child sign his name on his egg below the verse. Then instruct him to turn his egg over and decorate it with a variety of craft items, such as sequins, ribbon, glitter, and paint. It's a gift that would make any mother hen proud!

> Some eggs are green.
> Some eggs are blue.
> But this special egg
> Was made just for you!
>
> Love,
> Ben

Music and Movement Center

▶ counting down
▶ participating in a song
▶ rhyming

Cheep, Cheep!

Little fingers play a big part in this musical center. To prepare, cut apart the egg cups in a clean, sanitized egg carton. Then trim the top of each cup to look like a cracked egg and cut an X in the bottom of each cup. Put a supply of the finished egg cups in your music center along with a pad of washable yellow ink.

Teach youngsters the song below during circle time. Then invite each child to visit the music center to dramatize the song. To do this, a child pushes an egg cup on each finger of one hand and then presses the end of each finger into the yellow ink to resemble a chick. As each chick goes to sleep, the child removes one egg cup and folds that finger down. Sweet dreams, you tired babies!

Five Baby Chicks
(sung to the tune of "Five Little Ducks")

(Five) baby chicks hatched out one day.
Inside their nest they wiggled away.
With a peck, peck and a cheep, cheep, cheep!
One little chick fell fast asleep.

Repeat the verse for four, three, *and* two;
then sing the last verse (below).

One baby chick hatched out one day.
Inside his nest he wiggled away.
With a peck, peck and a cheep, cheep, cheep!
No one to play with, I might as well sleep!

TEC61183
TEC61183
TEC61183
TEC61183
TEC61183
TEC61183
TEC61183
TEC61183
TEC61183
TEC61183
TEC61183
TEC61183

Bunnies!

Hippity-hop up to learning fun with these bunny center ideas!

Bunny Bedtime

These little bunnies are hopping off to bed—in alphabet style! Use this adaptable center to address the needs of each of your children. To prepare, duplicate the bunny and basket patterns (page 75) on construction paper to make 26 of each. Write a different letter of the alphabet on each bunny and each basket. Adapt what each child will do in this center according to his abilities. For example, one child might match just five to ten bunnies to their baskets. Another child might put all the baskets in alphabetical order and match them up. Hippity-hop!

Literacy Center

▶ sequencing
▶ letter matching

Weighing Rabbit Food

Children will predict and verify which rabbit foods weigh the most, least, and just about the same. Put a variety of rabbit foods—such as carrots, green peppers, celery, broccoli, and lettuce—in a tub. Put the tub of foods in a center along with a balance scale. To do this activity, have a child select two different foods. Ask her to predict which food is heavier. Then have her use the balance scale to see for herself. If desired, ask each child to arrange the foods in order from lightest to heaviest.

Discovery Center

▶ tactile experience
▶ predicting
▶ weighing
▶ seriation

Bunny Hops

Math skills hop right along with this fun activity! In advance, take photos of classroom destinations (such as your water fountain or bookshelf) or make simple drawings of them. Stock a center with the pictures and a supply of paper and pencils. Ask children to visit this center in pairs. Have one person choose a classroom destination card and estimate how many hops it will take him to get from the center to the destination. Then have the child who drew the card hop to the destination while his partner helps count the hops. Then ask both partners to decide if the actual number was more than, less than, or equal to the estimated one. Then switch roles and continue in the same manner, hopping away!

Math Center

counting ◄
estimating ◄
measurement ◄
gross motor ◄

Hide-and-Seek

Prepare your sensory center for a little gardening by adding potting soil, child-safe gardening tools, and plastic veggies and flowers. Invite your students to set up the garden as they work in pairs. Then have one child hide a plastic Peter Rabbit toy somewhere in the garden. Can the other child (Mr. MacGregor) find Peter? Have the children switch roles and play again, taking turns with the gardening chores.

Sensory Center

sensory experience ◄
visual discrimination ◄
fine motor ◄

Carrot Painting

Carrots are not only for eating! Try using them in your art center! Stock a center with all kinds of carrots: whole, diagonal slices, and vertically cut sticks. Also provide some art paper and orange tempera paint mixed with a few drops of dishwashing liquid. Invite your students to hop on over and experiment making prints and pictures. For added discovery, provide yellow and red paint and encourage children to see what happens as the colors mix together!

Bunny Tails

Tempt your youngsters with these delightful bunny tail snacks! Give each child a five-inch circular doily. Position a rice cake in the middle of the doily. Have each center visitor spread whipped cream cheese on his rice cake and then add miniature marshmallows. What a cute, fluffy, and *tasty* tail!

It's Raining! It's Pouring!

Forecast a downpour of learning opportunities with these rain-related centers!

Literacy Center

- ▶ *vocabulary development*
- ▶ *word recognition*
- ▶ *print awareness*
- ▶ *writing and drawing*

Rain, Rain

Splash into vocabulary skills with this rainy-day booklet idea. In advance, make a blank booklet for each child by stapling together a copy of the booklet cover (page 79) and several half sheets of paper. Label each of several sentence strips with a different rain-related word and picture as shown. Display the strips at the center. If desired, decorate the center with a raincoat, rubber boots, and a child-safe umbrella. Invite each child to write his name on a booklet cover and then illustrate each rain-related word on a separate page. Encourage him to label each illustration by writing the corresponding word on the page. Invite him to take his booklet home to share with his family.

boots

rain

umbrella

puddle

cloud

boots

Math Center

- ▶ *nonstandard measurement*
- ▶ *estimation*

Buckets of Raindrops

Dip into estimation and measurement skills with a bucketful of raindrops! Copy the raindrop patterns (page 79) onto blue construction paper to make a supply. Cut the raindrops out and place them in a bucket at the center. Add an assortment of rain gear (hats, boots, umbrella) for the students to measure. Ask a youngster to choose one item and then estimate its length in raindrop patterns. Then have her measure the item using the raindrops. Buckets of fun!

Rain Repellent

Little ones will absorb the concept of water repellency with this investigation. In advance, gather an assortment of items for youngsters to test, such as newspaper, fabric squares, vinyl pieces, foam plates, and plastic sandwich bags. Program a chart as shown; then attach a sample of each item to a different column on the chart. Place the chart, test items, a container of blue-tinted water, and several eyedroppers at the center. Before opening the center, discuss the terms *absorb* and *repel* with your class. When a child visits this center, invite her to predict which items will absorb water and which ones will repel water. Then have her investigate by placing a few drops of water onto each item. Encourage her to record her observations on the chart as shown.

Does It Repel Water?					
Name					
Ashley	☹	☹	☺	☺	☺
Alex					
Jacob	☹	☹	☺	☺	☺
Sophie					

Science Center

observation ◄
predicting outcomes ◄
investigation ◄
fine motor ◄

Muddy Mystery

Mix up some marvelous, mushy mud for a great tactile experience! To prepare, partially fill your sensory table with potting soil. Half-fill a sprinkling can and a bucket with clean water. Gather several plastic items (counters, toys, balls) and several smocks. Then bury the plastic items in the soil so that your students do not see them. Tell your students that there is rainwater in the sprinkling can and bucket and there are mystery objects buried in the soil. Have each child at the center put on a smock. Ask one child to sprinkle the rain onto the soil as others observe. Then have each child use her hands to mix the mud. Encourage her to use only her sense of touch to guess the identity of an object she finds in the mud. Ask her to rinse her item in the bucket of clean water to clear up the muddy mystery.

Sensory Center

tactile investigation ◄
fine motor ◄
observation ◄

Motor Center

▶ fine motor
▶ creative expression
▶ hand-eye coordination

Drip, Drip, Drop

Create a shower of colorful raindrops one drip-drop at a time. In advance, cover a table with newspaper. Enlarge and copy the raindrop pattern (page 79) to make a class supply. Use red, blue, and yellow food coloring to tint three separate containers of water. Place the tinted water, three eyedroppers, and the raindrop patterns at the center. Have a child squeeze a drop of tinted water onto his raindrop. Model how to manipulate the raindrop to roll the droplet back and forth, creating a design. Then have him repeat the process with a different color. Set the raindrops aside to dry. If desired, display the rainbow raindrops for all to enjoy.

Art Center

▶ creative expression
▶ hand-eye coordination
▶ tactile experience
▶ fine motor

Fingerprint Showers

Sprinkle youngsters' creativity across these rainy-day illustrations. To prepare, gather a class supply of white paper, a supply of cotton balls, glue, crayons, and blue paint for the center. Invite each child to use crayons to illustrate an outdoor scene on her paper. Have her glue on cotton ball clouds. Then ask her to create a rain shower by adding blue fingerprints to her scene. Raindrops are falling!

Name _____

Raindrop Patterns

Use with "Buckets of Raindrops" on page 76 and "Drip, Drip, Drop" on page 78.

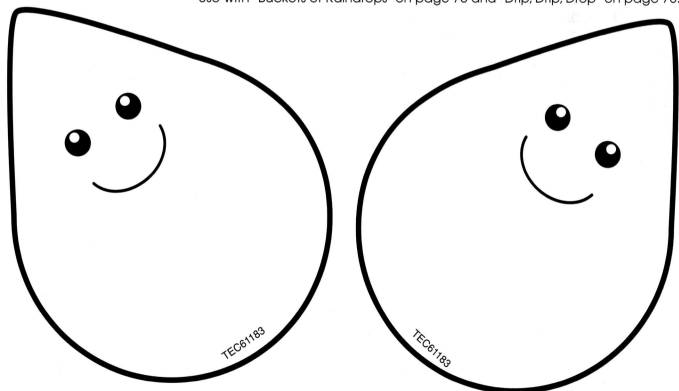

Invite your little ones to jump into these frog centers, which are hopping with curriculum-related fun.

**Math
Center**

▶ counting
▶ comparing
   quantities
▶ fine motor

FLIPPING FROGS

Youngsters will jump at the chance to complete this counting activity. To prepare, make a supply of frog manipulatives from plastic jug lids. Simply stick a frog sticker to the top (flat side) of each lid. Next, cut out a large lily pad from bulletin board paper and tape it down to the floor.

Have each child thumb-flip (or toss) the frogs onto the lily pad from a designated distance. Then direct her to count how many frogs land faceup and how many land facedown. Have the child compare the two quantities and determine which amount is greater.

**Science
Center**

▶ exploring magnets
▶ hand-eye
   coordination
▶ creative thinking

FROGS ON LOGS

Students exploring these magnetic frogs will discover that science is very attractive. Gather several miniature plastic or rubber frog figures. Hot-glue a magnet to the underside of each frog. Cut out a few lily pads from green card stock–weight paper.

Instruct a child to hold a magnet wand under the lily pad. Help him place a frog on top of the pad directly above the wand. Then have the child hold the lily pad with one hand and slowly move the wand with the other hand to manipulate the frog. Allow free exploration to see how many ways students find to move the frogs. It's an activity they're sure to stick with for a while!

LEAPING LILY PADS!

Hop into letter recognition and phonemic awareness skills with these linguistic lily pads. To prepare, cut a wedge out of each of five green paper plates. Program each plate with a different consonant: *d, f, h, j,* or *l.* Write the rime *-og* on a large index card. Spread the lily pads on the floor, post the card nearby, and provide a rubber frog toy or beanbag. To play, a child tosses the frog onto a lily pad. She then holds the designated lily pad next to the *-og* card, as shown, and reads the new word.

To adapt this idea for younger students, have children take turns tossing the frog and naming the letter (or giving its sound) on which the frog lands. They're learning by leaps and bounds!

Literacy Center

onsets and rimes ◄
letter recognition ◄
gross motor ◄

IN THE POND

Fill your sensory table with blue crinkled paper strips to represent water. Then add cardboard tube logs and craft foam lily pads. If possible, include a few dried cattails. Finally, gather a collection of frog toys—big ones, little ones, rubber ones, plastic ones, squeaky ones—and release them into this environment.

Invite visitors to the center to use the frogs to demonstrate positional concepts, such as *under* the water, *over* the lily pad, and *beside* the log. Then encourage students to play a quick game of hide-and-seek with the froggies. Be sure to also allow plenty of time just to let frogs be frogs!

Sensory Center

imaginative play ◄
position words ◄

Frog Fun

Give busy little fingers a workout with these dotty frogs. Stock the art center with a supply of sticky dots, hole reinforcements, construction paper, scissors, and markers. Invite each child to use the materials to create frogs in different colors and poses. Then have each child write or dictate the action in which each frog is engaged. Ready, set, stick!

Art Center

▶ creative expression
▶ fine motor
▶ vocabulary development

Frog Snacks

Getting a child to taste frog legs might be quite a feat, but you'll have no trouble at all convincing her to create and eat this funny frog. In advance, make a class supply of cupcakes without the icing. Duplicate the recipe cards on page 83. Color the cards and cut them apart. Post the cards in sequential order in your cooking center. Then arrange the ingredients and supplies listed below for easy student access. Invite each child to visit the center and follow the recipe cards to make a froggy snack.

Cooking Center

▶ following directions
▶ sequencing
▶ fine motor
▶ print awareness

Ingredients for one:
cupcake
green-tinted frosting
white candy wafer
2 chocolate chips

Utensils and supplies:
napkin (per child)
plastic knife (per child)

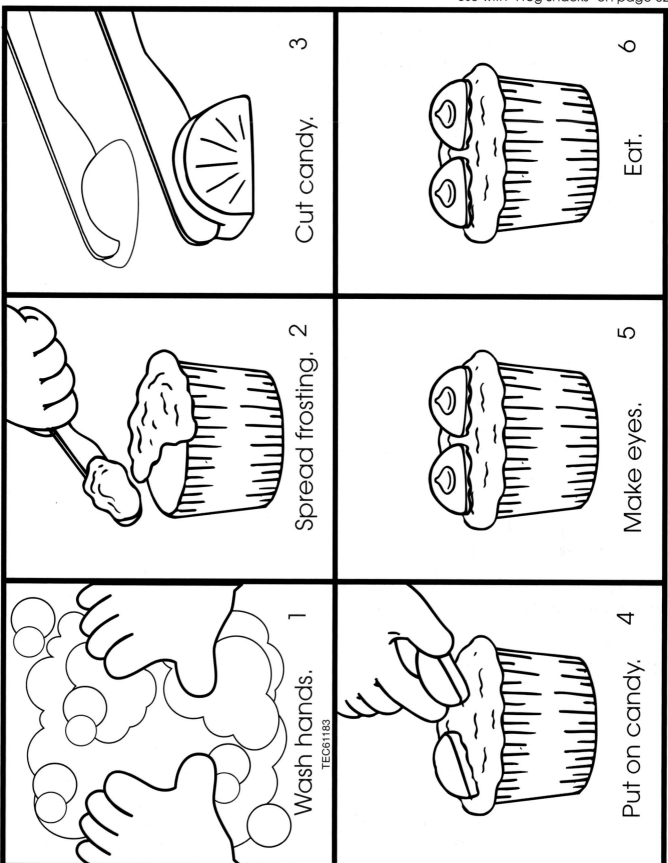

3
Cut candy.

6
Eat.

2
Spread frosting.

5
Make eyes.

1
Wash hands.

TEC61183

4
Put on candy.

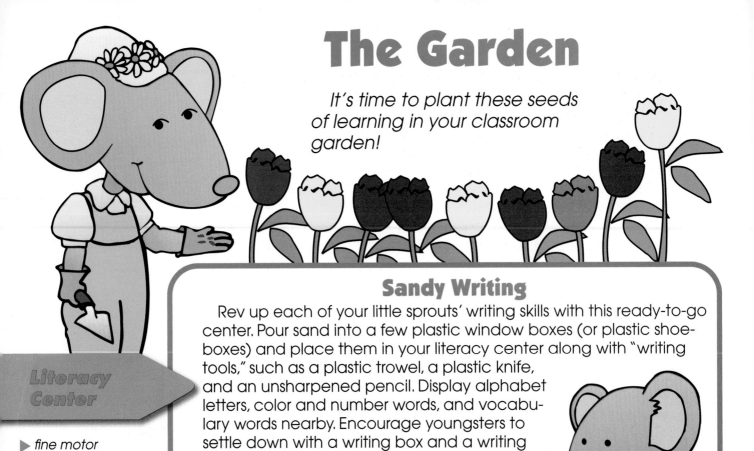

The Garden

It's time to plant these seeds of learning in your classroom garden!

▶ *fine motor*
▶ *writing skills*

Sandy Writing

Rev up each of your little sprouts' writing skills with this ready-to-go center. Pour sand into a few plastic window boxes (or plastic shoeboxes) and place them in your literacy center along with "writing tools," such as a plastic trowel, a plastic knife, and an unsharpened pencil. Display alphabet letters, color and number words, and vocabulary words nearby. Encourage youngsters to settle down with a writing box and a writing tool and write words and letters in the sand. Their writing skills will surely grow!

▶ *patterning*
▶ *fine motor*
▶ *creative expression*

Flower Power Patterning

Patterning practice has never been prettier! First, prepare a few homemade stamp pads by pouring different colors of paint into foam trays lined with paper towels. Provide strips of art paper and flower-shaped sponges (or cut your own shapes from sponges with a craft knife). Guide each child who visits this center in using the supplies to sponge-paint her own original patterns. When the paint is dry, invite children to describe their flower patterns during circle time.

Bird in the Garden

Little ones will love this cube puzzle game focusing on a legendary garden lover: a bird! In advance, wrap an empty tissue cube with paper. Next, reproduce the puzzle patterns (page 87) four times. Color, laminate, and cut apart all of the puzzle sets. Glue each piece of the fourth set to a different panel on the tissue box cube. To play this game, give one to three players a set of puzzle pieces. Have the first player roll the cube and find the puzzle piece from his set that matches the one on the top of the cube. He puts that piece in place to assemble his puzzle. If a player rolls a piece that he already has in place, continue play with the next player. The first person to complete his puzzle is the early bird!

Manipulatives Center

visual discrimination ◄
spatial awareness ◄
fine motor ◄

Garden Patch Visor

Youngsters will enjoy creating and wearing this visor that's just perfect for gardening! In advance, cut a class supply of nine-inch paper plates as shown in the illustration. Place the cut visors in your art center along with a supply of glue, silk flowers (stems removed), glitter crayons, construction paper scraps, ribbons, bows, and markers. Invite each child to decorate a visor as she wishes. When she's done decorating, loop two rubber bands together; then help her staple the looped bands to each end of the visor to get a perfect fit.

Art Center

fine motor ◄
creative expression ◄

Dramatic-Play Center

▶ *creative thinking*
▶ *role-playing*

"Kinder-garden"

Set up this garden center in a corner of your classroom and your little ones will be busy, busy in the garden! Pour a layer of potting soil or sand in a child's plastic swimming pool. Put it in a corner of your room. Then set up white picket fence garden edging along the walls. Add toy gardening tools, straw hats, and plastic fruits, veggies, and flowers. Include a few baskets so your gardening buffs can gather some of their own garden goodies.

Sensory Center

▶ *gross motor*
▶ *creative play*
▶ *hand-eye coordination*

Watering Day

A garden can't survive without water, and your water table is the perfect place for youngsters to practice the skills of not-too-much and not-too-little. Put a variety of watering cans in your water-filled table. Also add an assortment of waterproof toys—flowers, fruits, and vegetables would be perfect! Encourage children to explore using the different types of watering cans and trying to pour just the right amount of water over the toys.

TEC61183

Beautiful Butterflies

Flitter, flutter—your youngsters will glide through this collection of butterfly-related activities!

Literacy Center

▶ vocabulary development
▶ sequencing
▶ print awareness

Puzzle Poems

Piece together a poetic connection with this creative puzzle. To prepare, trace a large butterfly pattern onto a colorful sheet of tagboard. Cut it out and then cut it into three sections as shown. Write one line from the poem on each section as shown. Then lay the butterfly on a table and mix up the pieces. Read aloud the poem to your class. Ask each child at the center to sequence the lines of the poem, creating the butterfly shape. For a more challenging activity, ask youngsters to help create a poem to write on the butterfly.

Butterfly, way up high,

Flying in the clear blue sky,

Waving with a wing, "Good-bye!"

Math Center

▶ matching shapes
▶ symmetry
▶ visual discrimination

Symmetrical Patterns

Equally amazing! Youngsters will learn about symmetry as they match up this beautiful pattern-block butterfly. Make a class supply of the butterfly pattern on page 91 and place the patterns at a center along with a supply of pattern blocks. Invite each child to use a block to cover each corresponding shape on the butterfly. Encourage her to compare the butterfly wings, noticing they are exactly the same design and color. If desired, have her remove one block at a time and color each shape on her butterfly.

Butterfly Life Cycle

Youngsters will love the "pasta-bilities" of creating this model of the butterfly life cycle. Discuss with your students the stages of metamorphosis from a caterpillar to a butterfly. If desired, display books or pictures of the butterfly life cycle. Stock your center with a class supply of 2" x 8" tagboard strips and the following pasta types in various colors: orzo, spirals, shells, and bow ties. You may want to program each strip with the words "egg," "caterpillar," "chrysalis," and "butterfly." Invite each child to glue pasta onto his strip (and draw on details) to create the butterfly life cycle as shown.

Science Center

sequencing ◄
fine motor ◄

egg   caterpillar   chrysalis   butterfly

Fluttering Surprise

Pop, pop, pop! Crack the chrysalis to reveal a beautiful butterfly. Gather a class supply of short paper tubes and plastic straws. Prepare each tube by taping a three-inch circle of brown tissue paper to cover one end. If desired, have each child color or paint the paper tube brown or green to represent the chrysalis. Then make a three-inch butterfly tracer by drawing a simple butterfly shape onto tagboard. Ask the student to trace the butterfly shape onto white paper, decorate it, and cut it out. Tape the butterfly onto the end of a straw. Gently curl the butterfly wings inward and insert the straw into the open end of the chrysalis, butterfly end first. Encourage the student to explain the butterfly life cycle as he pushes the straw to help his butterfly emerge from its chrysalis.

Art Center

hand-eye ◄
coordination
following directions ◄
fine motor ◄

Motor Center

▶ fine motor
▶ hand-eye coordination
▶ patterning

Caterpillar Necklace

Improve fine-motor skills with these tasty caterpillar necklaces. In advance, gather a class supply of string licorice and fruit-flavored cereal loops (large and small sizes). Prepare each necklace by tying one cereal loop on one end as shown. Encourage each child to create a caterpillar by stringing cereal loops onto her necklace. If desired, have her reproduce a pattern you have specified. Then tie the ends together to make a wiggly necklace.

Cooking Center

▶ following directions
▶ fine motor
▶ tactile experience

Butterfly Snacks

This healthy snack is almost too cute to eat! To prepare, gather apples (half per child), bananas (quarter per child), chocolate chips, shredded cheese, vanilla yogurt tinted with food coloring, bowls, and a class supply of plastic spoons. Remove the seeds from the apple halves and place the halves in a bowl of water mixed with one tablespoon of lemon juice. Place the other supplies in individual bowls at the center. Have each child use his spoon to spread yogurt onto an apple and then place the banana in the center of it. Have him add chocolate chip eyes and cheese antennas. Decorate the butterfly wings as desired with chocolate chips or cheese. Yum!

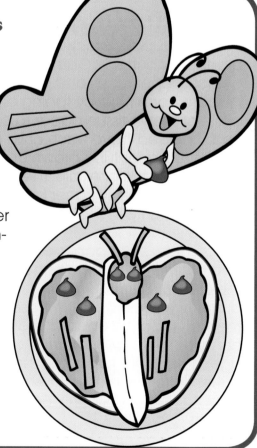

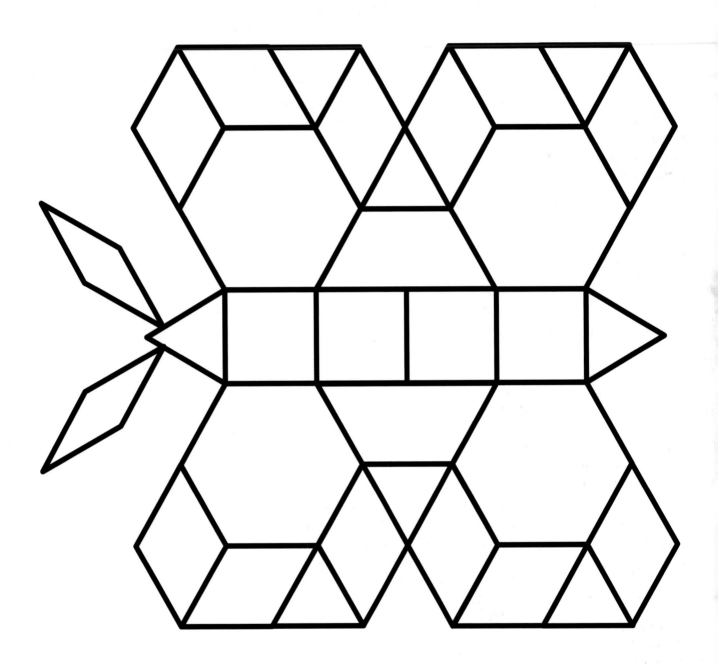

Note to the Teacher: Use with "Symmetrical Patterns" on page 88.

91

Pets

Unleash the fun of creative learning with these playful pet centers!

Motor Center

▶ fine motor
▶ classification
▶ sorting

Pocketful of Pets

Strengthen classification skills with this center. For this activity, you'll need two paper plate pockets. To make one, cut one paper plate in half. Align the front of a paper plate half along the edge of a separate whole plate. Staple along the edges through both plates. Label one plate "Pets" and the other "Not Pets."

Next, cut out a large variety of animal pictures from magazines. Glue each picture to a different index card. To do this activity, have a child look at each animal card and then place it in the appropriate pocket. Some of the animals might require a little extra discussion—according to your youngsters!

Tricks With Treats

Children will do all sorts of educational tricks with these treats! To prepare, fill a clean dog bowl with a variety of dog treats. When a child visits this center, encourage her to sort the treats by color, type, size, or any other attribute. If desired, encourage the child to use the treats to make a pattern, too. Good student!

Manipulatives Center

▶ sorting
▶ patterning
▶ visual discrimination

Pet Vet

Here's a chance to doctor up some creative thinking as well as lots of other skills! Stock your dramatic-play center with a variety of stuffed animals, gauze, cotton balls, stretch bandages, and cloth bandaging material. Also add notepads, pencils, and an appointment book. Invite children who visit this center to set up a veterinarian's office. Encourage them to play the roles of veterinarian, assistant, office staff, and clients. Make no bones about it—this is dramatic play at its best!

Dramatic-Play Center

creative thinking ◄
role-playing ◄
socialization ◄
writing ◄

A House for Me!

Block Center

fine motor ◄
creative thinking ◄
spatial awareness ◄

Architectural skills are front and center for this home-building activity! To begin, arrange a variety of different toy animals in your block center. Encourage each child who visits this center to design a house, pen, or crate for each of the different animals. Not too big. Not too small. Ah, this one is just right!

Literacy Center

▶ writing
▶ creative thinking
▶ socialization

"Paws-itive" Notes

Here's a pet-related twist to add to your writing center. Provide paw-print rubber stamps and stamp pads. (If you don't have rubber stamps that are appropriate for this, make a pawprint potato printer and have children use it with tempera paint.) In the center, also include pencils with pet designs. Set the tone for the center by adding pet-related books or even your live classroom pet. Encourage children to visit the center both to design stationery for general use and to write letters to classmates, school staff members, or people in their families.

Here, Doggie!

This little puppy is begging to help with math skills! In advance, cut out ten construction paper copies of the puppy and bone patterns (page 95). Write a different number on each puppy's tag. For each number, draw a corresponding dot set on a bone. To do this activity, have a child match each bone to a puppy. For variety, provide a supply of real dog biscuits and ask a student to give each dog the corresponding number of biscuits.

Math Center

▶ number recognition
▶ counting

puppy

bone

Goin' on a Picnic!

Celebrate the warm weather with these picnic-related center ideas.

Literacy Center

▶ print awareness
▶ visual discrimination
▶ memory
▶ turn-taking

Picnic Memories

This center game will get everyone in the mood for a picnic! To prepare, copy the pictures on page 99 twice. Color and cut apart the pictures; then glue each one onto a tagboard card. Laminate all the cards. Invite children to visit this center in groups of two or three. To play, have the children spread the cards on the floor facedown. In turn, have each player turn over two cards. If the cards match, he keeps them. If they do not match, he turns them facedown again. Continue play until all of the cards have been matched.

Manipulatives Center

▶ patterning
▶ fine motor

Picnic Patterns

The old-fashioned red-and-white checkerboard pattern still brings memories of summertime picnics. Encourage your children to design their own red-and-white patterns with this center idea. In advance, gather samples of the traditional red-and-white pattern on items such as napkins or tablecloths. Cut a large supply of small red construction paper squares and put them in a center along with white construction paper and glue. Then invite each child to visit the center and glue the red squares onto a white background to create his own red-and-white picnicky pattern.

You're the Cook!

Your dramatic little hams will love this center idea! To prepare, make a grill by stabilizing a cooling rack on top of a cardboard box. Then, using craft foam, cut out hamburger patties, buns, lettuce, ketchup, mustard, pickles, and onions. Put all the supplies in your dramatic-play area along with a spatula, a picnic tablecloth, and plastic place settings from your housekeeping area. When a small group visits this center, invite the children to take turns being the cook and the guests.

Dramatic-Play Center

creative thinking ◄
role-playing ◄
fine motor ◄
turn-taking ◄

Sink and Suds

Well, after the fun, there's always the cleanup. But even that can be fun in this center! Squirt some dishwashing liquid in your water table. Provide small rubber gloves if desired. Then ask children to gather the used plastic supplies from your classroom and wash them. Have one child wash and another one dry. Halfway through the job, ask them to switch roles. Now that's really sharing!

Sensory Center

sensory experience ◄
creative play ◄
socialization ◄

- spatial awareness
- creative expression
- fine motor

Picnic Pictures

These special projects will get your youngsters yearning for a real picnic! To prepare, stock your art center with a supply of white construction paper, assorted construction paper scraps, paintbrushes, and red and yellow tissue paper. Also fill empty ketchup and mustard squeeze bottles with slightly diluted white glue. When a child visits this center, encourage him to squirt several small puddles of glue onto his paper and use a brush to spread them out. Then have him press on red and yellow tissue paper pieces until the whole page is covered. Next, invite the child to use the construction paper scraps to design a large picnic entree such as a hamburger or hot dog. When his entree is complete, have him glue it to his red and yellow background.

The Ants Go Marching

The ants go marching how many by how many? Roll the dice to find out. To prepare for this center, color and cut out at least 12 copies of the ant pattern on page 99, then put them in your math center along with a pair of large dice, crayons, and a supply of paper that has been programmed with "The ants go marching ___ by ___." When a child visits this center, have her roll the dice to see how many ants will be marching on her paper. Encourage her to use the ant manipulatives to add the two numbers together. Then have her draw that many ants on her page and write that number in both of the blanks. During a group time, invite each child to share her page with the class.

The ants go marching 6 by 6.

- counting
- making sets
- addition

Picnic Pictures

Use with "Picnic Memories" on page 96. Also use the ant picture with "The Ants Go Marching" on page 98.

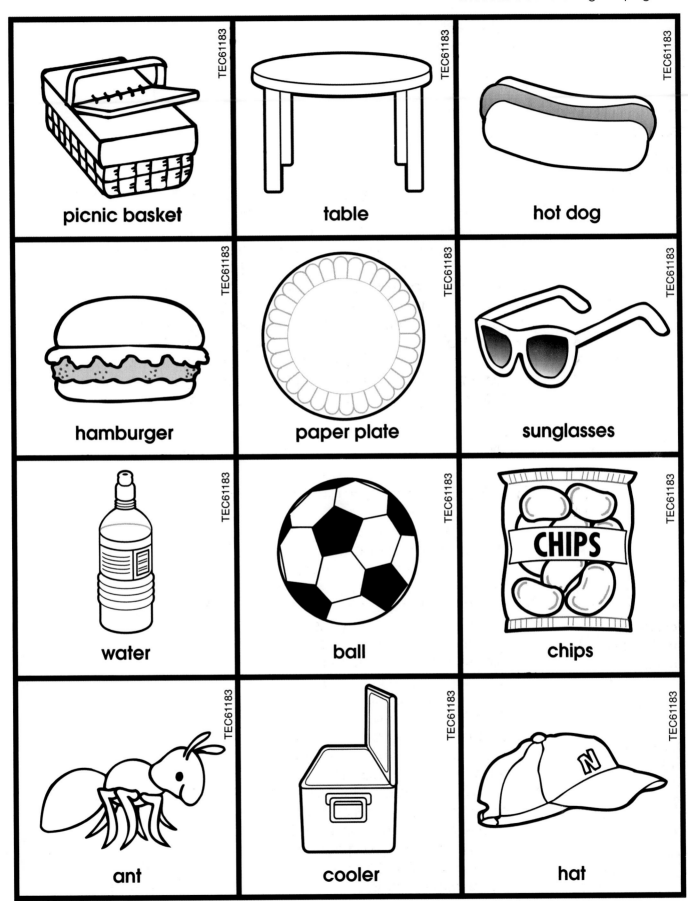

picnic basket

table

hot dog

hamburger

paper plate

sunglasses

water

ball

chips

ant

cooler

hat

Seeing Stars...and Moons!

These celestial centers will have little ones twinkling like stars and beaming like moons!

- ▶ *creative expression*
- ▶ *writing skills*
- ▶ *oral language*

Hey, Diddle Diddle

Youngsters' writing skills will take a jump at this center based on a favorite nursery rhyme, "Hey, Diddle Diddle." In advance, program a sheet of paper with the rhyme as shown. Then make a copy for each child. Place the copies at the center along with a supply of crayons and pencils. Invite each child to write her name where indicated on the paper and then draw a picture of herself jumping over the moon. When her drawing is complete, encourage the child to recite the adapted rhyme.

Hey, diddle diddle,
The cat and the fiddle,
Jessica jumped over the moon.
The little dog laughed to see such sport,
And the dish ran away with the spoon.

- ▶ *number identification*
- ▶ *counting*
- ▶ *number sequencing*

Star Struck!

You can count on this center to reinforce a number of basic math skills! To prepare, paint ten jumbo craft sticks with black tempera paint. When the paint is dry, use a white paint pen to program each stick with a different number from 1 to 10. Then add the corresponding number of foil stars to each stick as shown. Place the sticks in a container and set it at the center. To use the center, a child identifies the number on each stick, counts the stars, and then arranges the sticks in numerical order. Oh, my stars!

Sifting for Stars and Moon Rocks

Create pretend moon rocks for this center by rolling pieces of aluminum foil into balls. Bury the moon rocks in your sand table; then add a sprinkling of star-shaped confetti. Have each child use a sifter to search for the stars and rocks. One small step for teachers, one giant learning leap for students!

Sensory Center

sensory experience ◀
exploration and ◀
discovery
fine motor ◀

Reach for the Stars

Youngsters' creativity will be aglow when they make these collage stars. To prepare, cut out a black tagboard star shape for each child. Place the stars at your art center. Then add a supply of glittery collage items, such as pieces of aluminum foil, scraps of foil wrapping paper, and sequins. Have a child choose a tagboard star and then glue the collage items of his choice to one side of it. When the glue is dry, direct him to flip the star over and cover that side with the materials. Trim any excess material from the edge of the star, punch a hole in the top, and then thread a length of string through the hole. Suspend each child's star from the ceiling, and your classroom will look out of this world!

Art Center

creative expression ◀
following directions ◀
fine motor ◀

Motor Center

▶ fine motor
▶ creative thinking

Constellation Station

After showing students pictures of constellations, set up this center and invite each child to make a construction paper constellation. To prepare, gather a class supply of both white typing paper and black construction paper. Staple a sheet of typing paper over each sheet of construction paper. Place the stapled papers at the center along with a folded towel, a pencil, and an unused nail. To use the center, a child draws a simple design or writes her name in large letters on the typing paper. Under close supervision, she places her design on the towel and uses the nail to punch holes on the lines through both thicknesses of paper. Remove the staples from the papers. Discard the white typing paper, and then tape the sheet of black construction paper to a window. The light shining through the holes will make a stellar display!

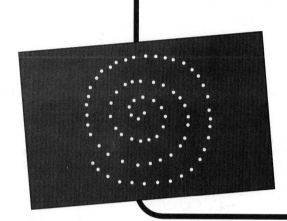

Cooking Center

▶ following directions
▶ measuring

Marvelous Moon Pies

Get ready for some moonlight madness at your cooking center! To prepare, photocopy the recipe cards on page 103. Cut out the cards and then display them in your cooking area. Next, gather the ingredients and supplies listed below and place them in the center. Encourage each child to follow the directions to make a lip-smacking snack!

Moon Pies

Ingredients for each child:
moon crater crust (miniature graham cracker crust)
½ c. of moonbeam (vanilla pudding)
1 tsp. moon rocks (granola)
dash of moondust (yellow sugar)

Supplies:
2 serving bowls
½ c. measuring cup
teaspoon
plastic spoon for each child
napkin for each child

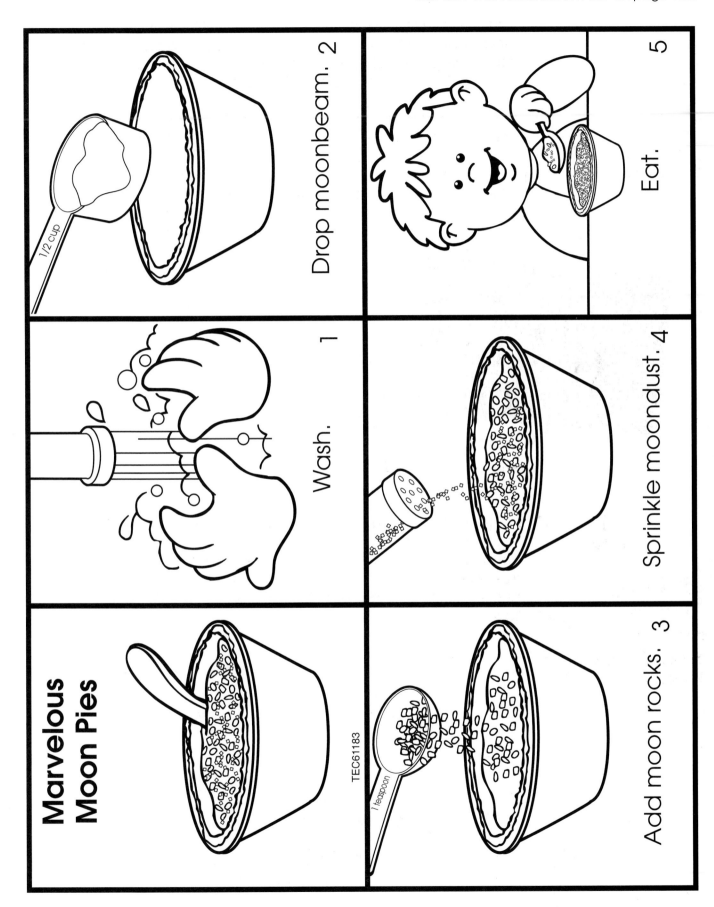

Marvelous Moon Pies

TEC61183

Drop moonbeam. 2

Wash. 1

Eat. 5

Sprinkle moondust. 4

Add moon rocks. 3

1/2 cup

1 teaspoon

"Zoo-bilee"!

Come join the fun as your students center on zoo animals. They'll have a squawking, squeaking, roaring good time!

Sensory Center

▶ sensory experience
▶ spatial awareness
▶ critical thinking
▶ counting

Wet and Wild

Gators, hippos, and crocs, oh my! Watch your little ones go wild with delight as they investigate zoo animals at the water table. To prepare, gather small toy zoo animals that enjoy the water such as alligators, crocodiles, hippos, seals, penguins, walruses, and turtles. Also cut some island shapes from cleaned and sanitized foam meat trays to float in the water. Invite the children to "swim" the animals through the water and then place them on the islands. How many animals can go on an island before it tips? Can you put more animals on the island if they're spread out or close together?

Motor Center

▶ fine motor
▶ spatial awareness
▶ sensory experience

On Behalf of Giraffes

Little ones will be stretching their necks to get to this center. In advance, cut out a yellow or orange construction paper giraffe for each child (pattern on page 107). Put the giraffe patterns in a center along with black markers, glue, brown yarn, scissors, and a shallow tray of brown tempera paint (with a few drops of dishwashing liquid mixed in if desired). Encourage each center visitor to use a marker to draw an eye and a mouth on his giraffe. Next, have him dip his index finger in the paint and then print spots all over the giraffe. To complete his giraffe, have the child squeeze a line of glue along the back of the giraffe's neck and then cut and attach short lengths of yarn to resemble the giraffe's mane.

No More Monkeys!

Many of your little ones know the popular rhyme "Five Little Monkeys Jumping on the Bed." This activity uses a zippy new zoo rendition! To prepare, duplicate the text box on page 107 five times. For each box of text, fill in the appropriate number; then glue each box to a different sheet of construction paper. Bind the pages in order between two construction paper covers; then title the book. Put the book in a center along with crayons, scissors, and a half sheet of white construction paper for each child.

Before children visit this center, teach them the rhyme below. Then encourage each child to visit the center to help illustrate a class book of the rhyme. Invite each child to draw and color a monkey on a half sheet of construction paper. Then have him cut out his monkey and find a place in the class book to glue it. It might go on one of the pages, on the cover, or on the endpapers. During a group time, share the book as your children read/recite the text!

Five little monkeys jumping at the zoo.
One fell down and cried, "Boo-hoo!"
The zookeeper said, "Oh, no! This just won't do!
No more monkeys jumping at the zoo!"

Free to Be

Many zoos are changing the layout of their "Zoo-villes." Instead of caging the animals, they are letting them roam free in a more natural habitat so that visitors can observe the animals as if they were in the wild. Use this center idea to illustrate how the old concept of caging animals at zoos is changing. In advance, gather white art paper, markers, paint (or stamp pads), and animal-shaped sponges (or rubber stamps). Demonstrate how to draw a fence using long horizontal strokes and then short vertical lines around the perimeter of the paper. Then invite each child to visit the center and make a fence around a sheet of art paper. Next, have him make prints of an animal inside the fence. When the paint is dry, display the paintings on a bulletin board titled "Free to Be."

- ▶ *counting*
- ▶ *graphing*
- ▶ *drawing conclusions*

How many zoo animals?

Count on the Zoo

In advance, prepare a graph similar to the one shown. Then pour a supply of zoo-type animal crackers in a large bowl. Put the bowl in your math center along with small paper plates, a marker, and sticky notes. Invite each child in the center to take as many animal crackers as she can in one handful and then put them on a plate. Have the child count the crackers and then write that number and her name on a sticky note. Then have her attach her sticky note to the appropriate place on the graph. Next, of course, is snacking! When center time is over, gather and discuss what the graph reveals.

Science Center

- ▶ *classification*
- ▶ *investigation*
- ▶ *critical thinking*

This Place Is a Zoo!

Invite your students to join you for a little "zoo-looking" at the science center. To set up special habitats, you'll need two deep trays or pans and a variety of small toy zoo animals. Also gather books and magazines that show the kinds of animals you've collected in their natural habitats. Arrange a layer of soil and grass in one of the trays; then pour water in the other. Invite your center visitors to place each of the animals in its natural habitat. Encourage children to support their choices with the books or other information they have learned about zoo animals.

Giraffe and Text Box Patterns

Use the giraffe with "On Behalf of Giraffes" on page 104 and
the text box with "No More Monkeys!" on page 105.

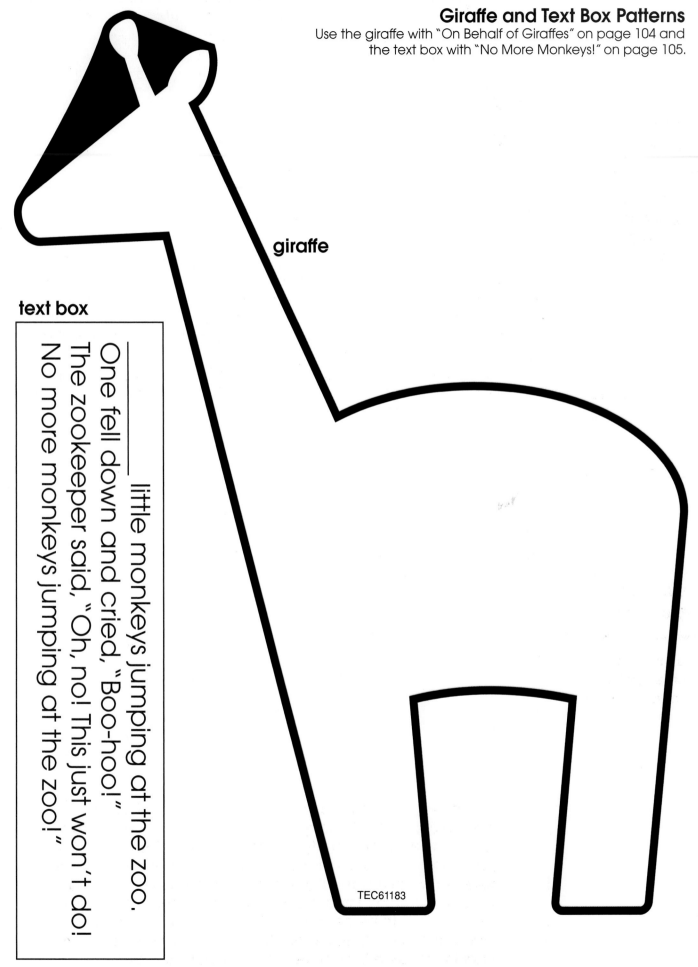

giraffe

text box

_____ little monkeys jumping at the zoo.
One fell down and cried, "Boo-hoo!"
The zookeeper said, "Oh, no! This just won't do!
No more monkeys jumping at the zoo!"

TEC61183

Teddy Bear Time

Your little ones will "bear-ly" notice they're reinforcing skills across the curriculum when they visit these terrific teddy bear centers.

Literacy Center

▶ matching uppercase and lowercase letters

Think, Think, Think

To prepare for this partner game, place a teddy bear and a set of uppercase and lowercase plastic letters at the center. Invite a pair of children to spread the letters on the floor. Have one child close her eyes while her partner hides a letter underneath the teddy bear. Then direct the first child to pick up the bear, find the hidden letter, and search for its matching uppercase or lowercase letter. The game continues in this manner until all the letters have been matched. For younger children, use two sets of uppercase letters.

Math Center

▶ counting
▶ making sets
▶ fine motor

Paws for Teddy

Count on this center to reinforce counting skills and "paws-itively" delight your little ones! Make several brown construction paper copies of the bear card pattern on page 111. Laminate the cards and display them at a center with large dice, play dough, and a supply of uncooked macaroni. Have each child flatten two small balls of dough and place one on each paw on her bear card. Next, instruct her to roll one die and push the corresponding number of macaroni into one paw to resemble the bear's claws. Then have her roll the die again to determine a number of claws to push into the second paw. Encourage her to remove the claws and play again for more "paws-on" counting practice!

Textured Teddy Tootsies

This matching activity gets your youngsters in touch with textures! Make two to four construction paper copies of the bear card pattern on page 111 and then laminate the cards for durability. Attach a small piece of self-adhesive Velcro® (hook side) onto each paw. Next, prepare sets of textured paws by cutting pairs of circles from various textures, such as sand paper, faux fur, felt, and corduroy. Then attach pieces of Velcro (loop side) to the backs of each pair. Hide one paw of each pair in the bag. To play, one child attaches a textured paw to a bear card. Another child feels inside the bag to find the matching paw and then attaches it to the bear's paw. Play continues until all the paws have been matched. Go ahead and touch those tootsies!

Science Center

tactile discrimination ◄
matching ◄

Please Feed the Bears

Invite your little ones to feast on visual discrimination skills at the bears' brunch! Simply add colored rice to your sensory table along with bear-shaped counters, pom-poms, sifters, and scoops. Invite little ones to stir, scoop, and sift. As children find the bears and pom-poms, encourage them to sort and count them into corresponding labeled bowls.

Sensory Center

visual discrimination ◄
color recognition ◄
sorting ◄
counting ◄

Bubbly Bears

These tactile teddy bears will quickly become the center of attention! Make a class supply of the teddy bear pattern on page 112. Next, tape 9" x 12" pieces of bubble wrap on a tabletop. Have each child paint a piece of bubble wrap with brown paint and then press his bear facedown onto the painted surface. Direct the child to gently lift his paper and then set it aside to dry. Finally, invite him to cut out his bear and use various craft materials to add desired details. Display these "grrrrreat" teddy bears for all to enjoy!

Art Center

▶ tactile exploration
▶ following directions
▶ creative expression

Teddy Bears on the Move

Teddy bears large and small enjoy moving to this familiar rhyme! In advance, color, cut apart, and laminate a copy of the word cards on page 111. Attach a small piece of Sticky-Tac® to the back of each card. Next, print the first verse of the teddy bear rhyme on a chart as shown. Then invite a student volunteer to choose a word card to place in the blank space on the chart. Have the students at the center recite and act out the rhyme. Repeat the activity with each of the remaining word cards. Teddy Bear, Teddy Bear, read and do!

Music and Movement Center

▶ gross motor
▶ following directions
▶ print awareness
▶ oral language

Teddy Bear, Teddy Bear,

 around.

Teddy Bear, Teddy Bear,

Touch the ground.

Teddy Bear, Teddy Bear,

Show your shoe.

Teddy Bear, Teddy Bear,

That will do!

Bear Card Pattern

Use with "Paws for Teddy" on page 108 and "Textured Teddy Tootsies" on page 109.

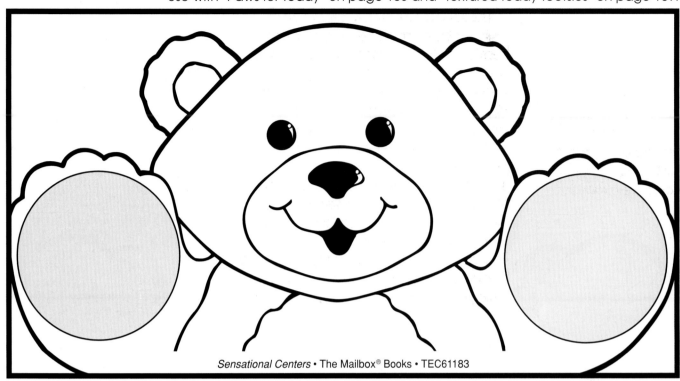

Sensational Centers • The Mailbox® Books • TEC61183

Word Cards

Use with "Teddy Bears on the Move" on page 110.

Turn

TEC61183

Stomp

TEC61183

Jump

TEC61183

Dance

TEC61183

Tiptoe

TEC61183

Run

TEC61183

Hop

TEC61183

March

TEC61183

Teddy Bear Pattern
Use with "Bubbly Bears" on page 110.

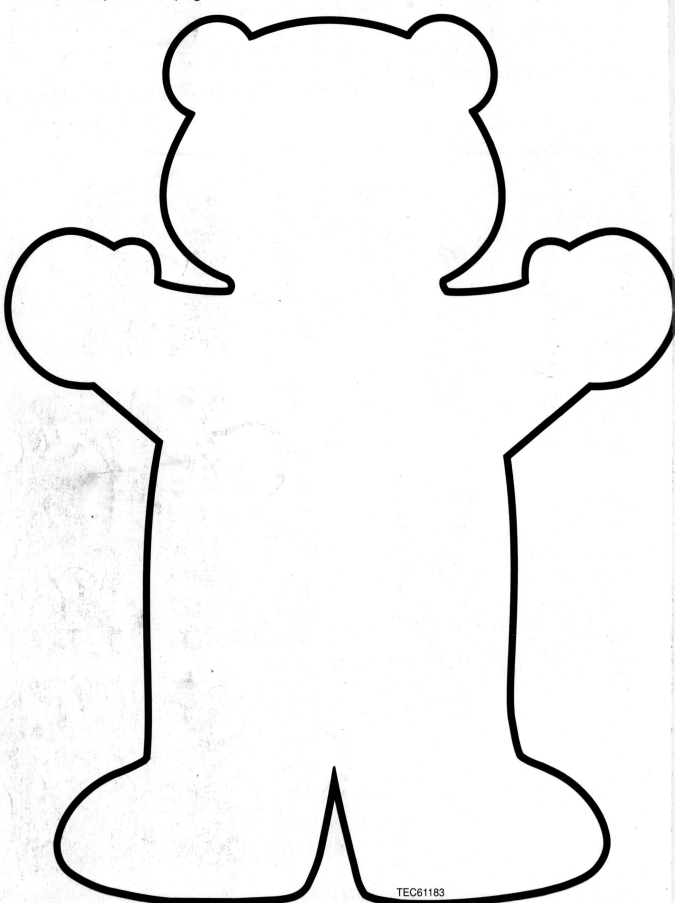

TEC61183